Silenced

Silenced

Vicky Jaggers
with Helen Roberts

HODDER

Publisher's Note
Names and locations have been changed throughout in order to protect the identities of individuals

First published in Great Britain in 2009 by Hodder & Stoughton
An Hachette UK company

1

A CIP catalogue record for this title is available from the British Library

ISBN 978 0 340 97677 7
Trade Paperback ISBN 978 0 340 97678 4

Typeset in Plantin Light by Hewer Text UK Ltd, Edinburgh
Printed and bound by Clays Ltd, St Ives plc

Hodder & Stoughton policy is to use papers that are natural, renewable and recyclable products and made from wood grown in sustainable forests. The logging and manufacturing processes are expected to conform to the environmental regulations of the country of origin.

Hodder & Stoughton Ltd
338 Euston Road
London NW1 3BH

www.hodder.co.uk

To Kirsty, Mum and Auntie Chris

ACKNOWLEDGEMENTS

I want to take this opportunity to thank Helen Roberts as without her help, support and caring attitude I would not have found the strength to be able to bring my life story to all you readers. I am eternally grateful as Helen had faith in me – as did my family, who are the ones I live for. They make life worthwhile and the past can fade easily when you have a future. I feel that now with my husband Kelly by my side, and my children and grandchildren around me, I can do anything. I would also like to acknowledge here how special my dad was. He will always be with me in my thoughts and in my heart.

Thank you to all at Hodder who helped make this book happen. I hope that my story will help others find the strength to deal with problems in their own lives.

CONTENTS

PROLOGUE

Sometimes it felt like I had disappeared behind the silence. My black, shameful secret had stolen everything from me. Other days it felt like life was so hard I would crack under the pressure and all that poison would come spilling out. What I did know, however, was that time was running out. He was getting more and more dangerous – more and more shameless in his violent deeds – and what I knew could put him away for ever.

The day before the trial was one of the hardest days I've ever had to face. Looking back, I imagine how different everything could have been if I had spoken up. But one look at Mum's face told me that would be impossible. There are some things that can never be unsaid, and there are some things a mother should never have to hear.

'For God's sake Vicky, he's family. You may never have been close, but he's your flesh and blood and we're all he's got.' She was standing at the kitchen window, staring out across the estate. 'It would mean so much for him to see you there.'

'Mum, I would, you know I would . . .' My heart was racing and my forehead was slick with sweat as I grasped for an excuse, but Mum was too wound up to notice.

'I've never understood why you two just couldn't get on. He must be so scared.'

'I'm just so busy with Kirsty now . . .' I trailed off feebly. She was starting to cry.

'Why don't they see it was an accident? Just a stupid bloody accident?'

I knew how much Mum loved David, but surely this court case had to make her realise what a monster her son was? How could she still love and trust in him now the whole world knew he had blood on his hands?

I wanted to shake her and hug her and argue her out of her love for him, but the only argument I could use was the one thing I'd vowed never to tell her.

It was years since I'd made that pact with myself. Back when my childhood was ripped away from me, I'd promised myself that no one else would have to suffer because of what David had done. Whatever happened, I would never let him tear our family apart.

But, while my family were all living a lie, someone got hurt – badly hurt. David had silenced Helen for ever. Would I really let him do the same to me?

I took a deep breath. For the thousandth time I wondered if I could find the words and break my silence. But a glance at Mum stole the words from my throat. She looked so fragile, like the slightest blow would knock her over. There was no way I could put her and my beloved dad through anything else. They had been through so much and I knew that my secret would break them. I'd unleash a storm of violence that would destroy everything that was good in our lives and crush it to dust.

So, yet again, I bolted the door where the truth was hidden and fumbled for an excuse.

'He's not going to be bothered about seeing me and Kirsty. As long as you and Dad are there . . . He's a big boy, after all.'

Mum looked at me full in the face. Had she seen something there? Had she suspected all along? Part of me longed for her to guess, to take this choking burden from my shoulders. For a moment it looked like she was going to question me; as if she had seen the dark cloud of the truth in my eyes and she was going to find out what was wrong. But it wasn't to be. With a sigh, she turned away, leaving me with my deadly secret once more. The conversation was over and I had failed us all again.

The trial lasted four nightmarish days. Mum was by David's side throughout, even acting as a witness for his defence. It tore me up inside to see her defending him. I only hoped that the judge and jury would see through the lies and realise what a dangerous man he was.

On the fourth day, I couldn't concentrate on anything. I kept picking up Kirsty's toys and moving them from room to room, waiting for Mum to come back and tell me the verdict. Still, I jumped at the sound of the keys in the lock. When they came in, Dad went straight upstairs without a word, without even looking at me. I poured Mum a cup of tea and waited with my heart in my mouth.

To start with, it was like she couldn't speak. I watched the tears roll down my mother's face, but I felt nothing. I just wanted her to speak up, to tell me the verdict. I felt like my whole fate rested in the words she was holding in. Anger and frustration burned in my stomach. The grey, shrunken ghost in front of me was a stranger. It seemed impossible that she was the same feisty woman who had been the darling of the bar room, mum to us all and David's staunchest supporter. The last few months had taken it out of her, and there were dark circles under her eyes. He'd done that to her. But it was nothing to the damage I could wreak if I just told her the truth.

Mum rubbed the knuckles of her left hand compulsively. I wanted to close my fingers over hers and still them, as if she was the daughter, and I was the mother who could protect her, who could magic away her pain. But, after all these years of bitterness and secrecy, I couldn't make myself touch her. She was the reason why David was still in my life. She was the reason why I'd never be free, whatever today's verdict.

My mother's eyes were bloodshot, and she was shaking, gulping the words out.

'He got eight years. Eight years.'

I watched as the tears began to stream down her face.

I nodded, eyes darting around the familiar furnishings of her cosy front room, desperately trying to avoid looking at her. I didn't want to read the anger and confusion scrawled over her face. Inside I just felt empty. I'd fantasised about this moment – being free of my brother and the guilty weight that had crushed my life – for years. What I would do. What I would say now that the world knew how evil he really was.

He had made something inside me die, and now there was nothing left – no pity, no warmth, not even a hunger for revenge. My mother's frame rocked with sobs, but I didn't go to her. I couldn't reach out to her. After years of keeping that terrible secret inside me, I hardly knew how to be a proper daughter. Even from prison, David was still coming between me and my mum, ruining our relationship, and that's something I could never forgive him for.

'Don't cry, Mum,' I said awkwardly.

'Sorry, love.' She wiped her eyes. 'You're right. We have to be strong for David. We'll appeal the verdict and soon we can be a proper family again.'

That's when I knew something for sure. My vile brother may have been sentenced to eight years, but my sentence would last much longer. There would be no early release for me, no freedom to look forward to, and, worse still, I would have to suffer in silence or risk the sanity and happiness of everyone I loved.

I

Early Days

Stretching out my arms and rubbing my eyes, I suddenly jumped up, threw my flowery pink duvet to one side and leapt out of bed. 'Dad!' I shouted. 'Where are you?' I heard him chuckling and found him in the kitchen, his arms flung out towards me. 'There you are,' I said, and I ran into them for a hug.

'What do you want to do today, then?' he asked. I looked at him excitedly; I knew he would have something planned. My dad, Len, always made me his priority. I was his special girl and every day with him was an adventure.

Most Saturday mornings in our council flat in Tilbury, I would look desperately for Dad in order to find out what he had planned for the day. I used to squeal with expectation, while Dad would sit back reading his newspaper laughing at my childish impatience.

'Well, go and get washed and dressed and I'll think of something,' he'd direct, and I'd race for the bathroom at top speed ... If it hadn't been for Dad, my childhood would've been very dull.

From as far back as I can remember, I was very close to my dad. He had such a loving nature and his hugs were so tight it felt like you were in the arms of a big cuddly bear. He was quite a slim, lanky man, though, and he seemed much younger than most grown-ups. When me and my siblings were born, he was still only young, but he took to fatherhood

to family legend. My dad may not have
.e a bear, but still, his hugs were so cosy
And I've been told many times by members
nat Dad was besotted with me from the day I
athing me and changing my nappy as soon as I
. from hospital. In fact, he was much more hands-
on ti. i my mum ever was. She was exhausted after the
birth and also had the other kids to worry about.

My mum, Avril, was a very bubbly blonde and she
loved a good time. She was petite, like my dad, and very
attractive. I thought she was absolutely beautiful and
looked up to her like crazy. Although I know she loved
me, Mum didn't always know how to show it. She would
sometimes walk away as I was trying to tell her one of
my long, childish stories, distracted by a magazine on the
kitchen table or a shout from the street. Mum always made
time for my elder brother, David, but she just wasn't really
a girl's girl. Dad sometimes warned her against playing
favourites, though, so she would then make a real effort to
take an interest in me too.

Mum was a few years older than my dad and didn't
have so much time to spend being silly with me. She was
a working mother, and was often worn out; although she
made sure she enjoyed life too, and always had a noisy circle
of friends. When I was about five years old, we moved to a
house on Bata Avenue, near the Bata Shoe Factory, in East
Tilbury, Essex. Dad was already working there as a welder
and then Mum got a part-time job as an assistant in the
factory itself. I remember Mum and Dad getting really
excited, because, with them both working there, we'd be
eligible for a family house on the factory site, which meant
a way out of our cramped, three-bedroom council flat,
which barely fitted us all inside.

We were quite a big family, and not an altogether straightforward one, but then, of course, most families have their quirks. I was the baby of the household – the youngest of four children. I was never very close to my oldest brother, John Paul, who was almost ten years older than me. He was far happier spending time with his friends and messing around on his CB radio than hanging out with his kid sister.

I also had an older sister, Tina, but she didn't live with us. She was eight years older than me and had fallen off a high chair before I was born, leaving her with behavioural problems. As she got older, she became a real handful for Mum and Dad. She was very violent, especially with Mum, who sometimes had cuts and bruises all over her face after Tina's outbursts.

Apparently, when I was just a baby, Tina tried to strangle John Paul while in a temper and he passed out. Mum had had to lock Tina in the bedroom while she tried to resuscitate John Paul. Consequently, my parents had a very difficult decision to make about her future with the family, but, in the end, they had to face the fact that Tina's temper was endangering everyone – including herself – and they arranged for her to be sent to a special school.

So, while I was growing up, Tina was away a lot, either at boarding schools for special pupils or in care homes. When she occasionally came home for a weekend or a holiday, I used to always feel a bit scared of her. When I was a very small child, I remember feeling uncomfortable around Tina because she was so different from the rest of us. Now I'm older, I hate to think of how lonely she must have felt, but back then I was too young to understand. She was very disruptive and I found it hard to relate to her as one of the family. Looking back, I can see that my mum really missed Tina. Perhaps that's why she focused so much attention on David? It was as if she thought pouring her love into him would help her forget about his sad, troubled older sister.

I was closest to David, who was five years older than me and a typical 'big bro'. When I was born he was apparently completely obsessed with me and was always kissing me and stroking my head. As I grew up, he was very protective of me, sometimes overly so. Even then he was a smart little boy, and my mother worshipped the ground he walked on. While she could be very distant with me, she was always fascinated by David, always asking him what he'd been doing and who he was friends with. And he already had an uncanny ability to charm people, so there were always lots of new friends for him to tell Mum about.

As I got older, Dad and I became closer and closer and I followed him everywhere. Sometimes I'd go to work with him, while other days we'd go out in the car, fishing or bug watching in the nearby fields. I was his little princess, and I looked like him too, with wide eyes and a broad, infectious grin. On the other hand, everyone said the boys were the spit of their mother, with their blonde hair and striking pale eyes.

I was a typical tomboy – most people said I should've been born a boy – and I loved to be involved in everything Dad did. Wherever we went, people would call out to my dad 'You all right, mate?' as we walked down the street, and I felt so proud of him and how popular he was. I wanted to shout from the rooftops: 'This is my dad and he's all mine!'

Honest and hard working, Dad tried to provide for us and secure a nice life. He tried his hand at many jobs over the years, but was generally a welder by trade. Coming from Essex, it was a typical male job, but, considering he was a slim, wiry man, it was surprising he did such physical work. He was always smartly dressed though, and his full head of brown hair was always well cropped to shape his strong, thin face. Dad was a good-looking man, but he could never get over his luck in getting a gorgeous woman like my mum. Whenever any of the neighbouring women flirted with him, he laughed and thought they were only teasing him. With Mum so busy with David, I had a lot of time to devote to being his biggest fan.

Although Dad worked long hours, he always seemed to have plenty of time for me. He usually had his work gear on most days, and whenever I was close to him I'd breathe in big lungfuls of his smell. He had a musty, working man's smell, which lots of people probably would have found unpleasant, but I loved it because it belonged to him.

The Bata Shoe Factory site, where we now lived, was like a little village for the factory's workers. The company had created a little community, with a school, shops, cinema, hotel and a swimming pool – it was great, completely different to the rough estates my parents were always trying to get us away from.

Mum usually worked from 9am to 3pm, Monday to Friday, and so she was always at the school gates when we got let out, waiting to take us home and cook our dinner. Our house was always filled with delicious cooking smells, as Mum loved to experiment with different dishes – although her favourite meal, which was our favourite too, was good old-fashioned stew and dumplings. It was gorgeous.

It was important to my parents that we ate dinner at the table together every night. We had to be clean and sitting down by 6pm. And Mum used to always overcook, in case someone called round, or my brother's friends were in the area and needed feeding. I wasn't as sociable as my siblings and consequently rarely had any dinner guests, but my brothers had big groups of friends who were always round, and both Mum and Dad loved to welcome them to the table. 'Are you joining us tonight boys?' Mum would ask as she was serving up. 'Is that OK, Mrs J?' the boys would ask, then come running over and start eating like vultures.

I do remember one day, when I was about six, David eleven and John Paul sixteen, that it was just the family for once. Mum had cooked an enormous cottage pie and John Paul leapt on it as soon as she set it down.

'Off, you!' she said, batting John Paul with her oven gloves. 'Leave some for the rest of us. David hasn't had any yet, and he's a growing boy.'

Dad and I caught each other's eye across the table and laughed. Mum was so predictable.

'Fine, go on then!' John Paul muttered sulkily.

David smirked. 'There's no reason to behave like an animal, just because you're a moron.' John Paul looked like he'd like to punch his little brother's lights out.

'Shut up, David, and pass it here. Mmmm, looks delicious,' Dad said, wanting to avoid a fight.

I wanted to ask what a moron was, but John Paul was glowering enough already. David didn't seem to notice the bad atmosphere. He was funny like that. He'd wind someone up and then be really surprised if they got annoyed at him. Of course, it was different the other way round. Even as a little boy, David would fly off the handle at a moment's notice, lashing out until he'd hurt or humiliated the other person. So, even then, I was careful to stay on his good side.

I hated my family to argue, so, out of nowhere, I started telling this long rambling joke I'd heard from one of Dad's friends. Of course, I was too young to remember it properly, so I kept on getting mixed up. It was so silly that everyone started laughing, even John Paul. My mum even gave me an extra dollop of ice cream and it felt like we were a happy, close-knit family again.

David and I were at school together for about a year before he went up to secondary school. This was about the time, when I was around five or six, that I started to really struggle at school. Mum eventually took me to see a specialist and, after a few tests, I was told I was dyslexic. But, when the other kids at school found out, I was called 'thicko' and chased around the playground. School became a nightmare for me.

Once, a group of older kids cornered me in the playground. It was the start of lunch break, and all the teachers were still in the dining room. I looked around, but there was no one to help me.

'I know you,' a big ginger-haired boy said, looming towards me and jabbing a finger in my chest. 'You're the retard.'

His friends sniggered behind him. When I didn't respond, he snatched my satchel from me.

'You can have it back if you can spell it out for me.'

'Give it here!' I yelled, making a grab for it. The boy chucked it to his friends and shoved me off balance. We'd bought the bag in town only last Saturday. My parents would kill me if anything happened to it.

'Come on, thicko, I'll help you out,' he taunted. By now quite a crowd had gathered. They were all waiting for me to respond. I saw David on the outskirts of the crowd, which made me feel even more pathetic. My clever big brother would never get himself in this situation, and now he'd tell my mum all about it and they'd laugh at me too. At that thought, I couldn't hold back the tears any longer.

'B . . .'

One of the girls held my bag upside down and I saw my purple pencil case smash open on the floor.

'A . . .'

The ginger-haired boy came up close to me again. I could smell onions on his breath and I couldn't stop crying.

'G . . .'

Suddenly there was a shout, and out of nowhere there was David, storming towards the boy.

'Oi, what do you think you're doing?'

He was shouting at the top of his voice. Unlike me, who was small for my age and shy with it, David was a threatening presence in school and all the kids were on edge around him.

I crept off to into a corner, happy, this once, to let David take centre stage yet again. 'Do you like picking on my little sister, do you? Well, what about picking on me?' he snarled.

The red-haired boy didn't want to lose face in front of his cronies, so he took a swing at David. That's all my big brother was waiting for. He ducked the clumsy punch and kneed the bully hard in the stomach. As the boy staggered over, David continued to kick him, even when he was lying on the floor and all his so-called mates had run away.

I couldn't watch and ended up creeping away. I never particularly wanted him to fight for me – I didn't even like fighting – but it seemed to be his way of expressing how he cared about me.

David himself was certainly never called 'thicko'. In fact, it soon became pretty clear that he was incredibly intelligent. His teachers at school often called Mum and Dad in for meetings about his capabilities. He could complete tests in minutes, and almost always get 100 per cent without even trying. Some years later, when David was a teenager, he had a test at school and apparently he had an IQ of 153. Since the average score is 100, that made him exceptional, especially considering the rough schools he'd gone to. It was generally agreed that he was a gifted child who had extraordinary abilities.

One day it finally hit me how talented David was. I was in his room one afternoon watching him play with some discarded computer parts. 'What are you doing David?' I asked. He just looked up at me silently and carried on. I sat on his bed and watched in astonishment as he created a carousel out of random parts lying around his room. 'Wow, that's amazing!' I squealed, as I twirled the intricate structure round and round. Despite his previously off-hand manner, David looked chuffed that I had admired it. I took it to my room and cherished it, showing it to anyone who visited. During those early years, I suppose Mum and Dad were pleased their children got on, especially David and me. From the outside, David came across as a typical big brother, not being over the top but showing me enough attention to make me feel important.

For me it was a bit more complicated than that though. We never talked about it again, but that day in the playground stayed with me for a long time. On the one hand, I was shocked by how violent David could be, but on the other hand I was strangely proud of him, and very grateful to him for saving me from the bullies. I was also glad that he never mentioned anything to my parents. I was so embarrassed at looking like a stupid victim. Most of all, I reckoned I owed him one. From then on I tried to ignore his strange ways and focus on the positive aspects of his personality. That's what made his betrayal of me so terrible in the end. As it turned out, I had so much more to fear from him than I ever did from some ignorant playground thug.

2

Moving On

My fondest memories of my childhood are of the holidays we spent together as a big family at Lambeach Marina Caravan Park, in Cambridgeshire. It'd be Mum, Dad, David, John Paul and me, as well as Dad's sister, Aunt Chris, with her husband, and my cousins Kate and Kayley. We'd go whenever we could afford it – summer, Easter and Halloween, or even long weekends. It was only at Christmas and New Year that we stayed at home, because Dad loved family Christmases so much. Looking back, it's obvious that something was worrying my parents. Whenever we were at home there'd be weeks of whispered arguments and slammed doors. But, as a kid, all I focused on were these holidays, where Mum and Dad would relax and start talking normally and laughing again, and I'd play endless card games with my brothers and cousins.

The caravan park we went to was gorgeous, surrounded by lakes, fields and forests. It had a tent and caravan field, as well as room for static caravans. There were three bars for the grown-ups and a café where us kids could hang out. I loved it. We stayed in a caravan we owned at the time and we also put up a few tents. David and the boys loved the freedom of being out in the tents, while the rest of us slept in the caravan. I spent all my time with my cousin Kate. Everyone said we were like Laurel and Hardy, and we always had such fun together. Kate was my age, but shorter than me, with brown frizzy hair that stuck out at all angles. She always looked comical, like she was just about to laugh, and her pretty looks often got her out of trouble. Even at that age I was quite shy and didn't like speaking up for myself, but Kate was always loud and cheeky, so we must have made quite a contrasting double act. But Kate was really kind too, and I thought the world of her. As she was also family, she was different to other friends and so I never felt self-conscious or nervous around her.

I remember us all having a lot of fun together at the park. Once there was a water festival on the lake and there were specialist water skiers who did stunts. It was amazing; completely different from anything I'd ever seen. The skiers were so free when they jumped over the water. It was like nothing could hold them down.

As part of the festival, there was also a man going round in a monkey suit. David thought it was hysterical, but as soon as Kate spotted him, she ran a mile, completely petrified. We all spent hours trying to find her because she had just bolted and fled. It was so unlike my loud, confident cousin that the adults were laughing about it, but as we searched all over the park I started to worry that something had happened to her. In the end, we found her safe and sound, hiding under her duvet back in the caravan. Turned out my brave cousin Kate had a vulnerable side to her after all. After that day she carried on as if nothing had happened and never wanted to talk about why she had been so scared. In our family we respected each other's space, so I never pried into her silence; just as – a few short years later – no one would pry into mine.

It was not long after we returned from the park that time that something went badly wrong with our family. It seems that Kate wasn't only the only one who'd been keeping her cards close to her chest. I should have guessed from all the tension in the house that Mum was seriously worried, but at the time I was only nine years old; I had complete faith in my parents being able to preserve my happy, safe little life and, of course, I always wanted to believe the best in people.

One afternoon, Mum came back from her job at the Bata Shoe Factory with a white face and red eyes. As soon as she was inside the house, she pulled Dad into their bedroom and shut the door. They started talking in low, serious voices, and I couldn't make out what they were saying. My heart was in my mouth. What could have happened? Was she sick? Why didn't they want me to hear? I knew something was badly wrong because on the way up the stairs Mum hadn't even asked where David was, like she usually would. Even though it annoyed me that David was her favourite, it hurt much more to think of something bad happening to my beautiful mum.

It seemed a long time before Mum and Dad came out of the bedroom and sat me down.

'Now, love,' my Dad said, stroking my hair. 'We've got some news.'

'What sort of news?' I asked. My mother looked like she was trying not to cry.

'We're moving, Vicks. We're packing up. Going on an adventure.' Dad was trying to smile.

'Oh, OK,' I said slowly. 'What about Kate? Is she coming too?'

'No. She'll be staying with Auntie Chris. We can come back and visit her. It'll be OK,' he murmured, seeing my bottom lip starting to tremble. 'You can play with your brothers instead. The family will be together, and that's all that matters.'

'But why—' My mother cut me off, maybe a bit more harshly than she intended.

'Vicky, I lost my job. We're leaving. You'll be fine. I really don't want to hear another word about it.' With that she strode off to find David and I hid myself in Dad's warm arms, which always felt like home. As long as I had him, I knew I'd be OK.

Looking back, I'm glad I was too young to realise what a bad situation we were in. We'd never had a lot of money, but Mum's redundancy made it impossible to make ends meet. While I was fretting about my little life being turned upside down, my parents were struggling to put food on the table. The arguments in the bedroom became more and more frequent and we lived off egg and chips for weeks.

After Mum was laid off we went back to the caravan park for two weeks, and in that time Mum and Dad decided to make a fresh start and move to the area permanently. I was thrilled; it felt like a permanent holiday. It was a fresh start and living in a caravan park seemed, to a nine year old, like the best news ever. Dad got himself a new job and we made the caravan park our home. After the novelty wore off, though, I realised it wasn't the same without my cousins. I missed Kate for a long time and longed to see her. I'd sit in my room wondering what mischief she was getting up to.

'C'mon, Vicky,' Dad would say. 'Cheer up.'

'I don't know why she's being such a sulky mare,' David would grunt from his bunk.

'Well, it wouldn't kill you to spend a bit of time with your sister . . .' Dad replied.

'It might do, you know,' David retorted, his voice muffled by his duvet. 'Or I might end up killing *her* if she doesn't stop whining.'

'Vicks, get out of your brother's hair, please.' Mum's voice cut in from the kitchen, and Dad would roll his eyes and take me off to the park.

I can imagine the disruption would be hard for some kids my age, but I was determined to make the best of it and not worry my parents.

We all lived squashed together in our old caravan until Mum found a job as a cleaner and the caravan park's manager's wife, who was an estate agent, managed to find us a house to rent not too far away, in Meeple. I was relieved to have my own room again. David could be so moody and unpredictable that I had started to dread sleeping together in such a cramped space. But away from the caravan my unease quickly melted away and the redundancy was soon a distant memory.

I loved our new home and when I joined Meeple Primary School I soon made some friends. As usual, I wasn't the most sociable kid in the class, but there was this one girl, Alice, who was really friendly. She was quite shy and I don't think she had many friends either, so we actually had something in common.

'Do you want to come for dinner tonight?' Alice asked one day. 'Mum said it was OK and we've got lots of animals.' I loved animals and soon I was going back to her house after school most evenings.

Alice and her family lived on a farm, just down the road from our house, so it was really easy for me to get home afterwards. We watched TV together and went for walks. The farm had pigs and cows and stables with horses in them. Alice was an amazing horse rider and every time I saw her ride I was in awe of her. We became very close, and she taught me to ride too. Apart from my Dad, I wasn't used to people being affectionate with me. It was always my clever, charming older brother they wanted to talk to.

Alice had an older brother, Stephen, and he used to hang out with us sometimes. For me it was a real eye-opener to see how well Stephen and Alice got on. There was never any strange atmosphere between them. Alice and Stephen teased each other mercilessly, but there was never anything dark or nasty about it, and their fights were never more than play fights. I wished David and I could have had such an easy relationship.

With Alice as my best friend, and my newfound obsession with riding, I blossomed into a happy, busy little girl. I would have loved to have stayed in Meeple for ever. Even the school wasn't too bad! Perhaps, if we had stayed somewhere where I had real friends, ones I could trust, everything would have been different. But this beautiful and exciting life was to be short-lived. Less than two years in, my parents broke the news that we had to move again. I nodded stiffly, went up to my room and cried and cried. When I look back, those years in Meeple were the happiest years of my life.

Although I was sad to leave Meeple, my dad soon made me see that it wasn't the end of the world.

'You'll make new friends, love,' he said, looking down anxiously into my face. 'And, anyway, isn't the most important thing that we're all together? Friends come and go, but family is for ever.'

'I suppose so,' I said, trying to smile for him.

'That's more like it.' Dad gave me one of his big soppy grins. 'We'll have lots of good times together in the new place. You'll see . . .'

That night I went to bed with dry eyes. Dad was right – my family was all I needed. They'd look out for me.

Little did I know then that my ideas about my perfect family were based on fantasy, and that the whole façade would soon come crashing down.

3

Warning Signs

By the time I was ten, I had begun to realise that our family structure wasn't what it seemed. I'd always known that Mum adored David, but I'd just reacted by turning into a total daddy's girl. So when Mum and Dad started snapping at each other, I couldn't help taking sides. I don't know if I had just been too young to notice it before, but after we left Meeple they just didn't seem to get on any more. While I felt sorry for Dad, and I could see how devastated he was by all the rows, David grew closer to Mum. It felt like the whole family was splitting in two. In Meeple, I'd been so caught up with my friends and my own happiness that I had been able to ignore the warning signs. Now that I was spending all my time with my family again, I couldn't stop worrying that something awful would happen. I reacted by retreating into myself. If I was a good, quiet girl and didn't bother anyone everything would be all right, wouldn't it?

After we left Meeple, we moved to a new house in Chittering and life seemed to go on as always. I kept out of everyone's way, and tried to ignore the shouting. I also acted the peacemaker, calming David down when he went off on one, and trying to make my parents laugh. My tactics seemed to work . . . for a while.

But one morning I woke up, hopped over to the kitchen as I did every morning, and noticed something was different. The atmosphere felt weird. I looked around trying to determine what had happened, and then it sunk in – Dad wasn't there. I went to my parents' bedroom and all his things had gone. It felt like someone had hit me in the stomach and bile rose suddenly in my throat. I was sick with panic. I raced round the house frantically looking for any sign of him, but everything was gone – clothes, shoes, coat. Like a puppy that'd lost its master, I was lost and desperately confused. I hadn't heard Mum and Dad arguing last night, but gradually my instincts told me what had happened; I knew Dad had left us, but I just didn't want to believe it. Like a robot, I made myself some breakfast and waited for Mum to come in and offer another explanation, one that meant my family hadn't been torn apart.

Mum didn't look at me as she walked into the kitchen.

'Where's Dad?' I asked, stirring my bowl of cereal with my spoon. I looked up at her for a minute, hoping she'd crack and spill everything out.

'Vicky . . .' She sounded tired, and I knew she wanted me to leave it, but this was important.

'He's supposed to take me fishing. He promised.'

She was silent, methodically washing up last night's dishes and putting them away. Maybe she hadn't heard me over all that banging? I tried again. 'Mum. Has Dad left? When's he coming back?'

She swung round and, for a second, I thought she was going to tell me what was happening. But, quick as a flash, the shutters came down and she turned away from me again.

'C'mon, eat your breakfast,' she said coldly. 'I can't stand around here all day.'

'Mum . . .' I said, pleading with her, but she refused to even look at me again.

That was it; that's all the explanation I was given for my dad leaving. I couldn't believe it. Of course, Mum must have been hurting too, but the message from her was very clear: shut up and put up. That's one lesson I never forgot. So, even though my darling dad was gone, I didn't let myself cry. Instead, I watched Mum clear the kitchen like nothing had happened. I couldn't help but feel bitter towards her. Why couldn't she reach out to me, put her arm around my shoulder like she did with David? But that was Mum. She always presented a tough front, even when I was desperate to see her softer side. My family was falling apart, and Mum made it all too clear that she was the last person I could turn to for comfort.

My heart felt like it had fallen to my feet for the rest of the day. I couldn't imagine our home being the same without Dad around. I carried on eating my breakfast that morning with tears in my eyes, but I was determined I wouldn't let them fall. Dad was the one who kept us all together. Mum was the type of parent who thought children shouldn't know what adults got up to; that they should mind their own business. Because I loved Dad so much I became very angry with Mum and blamed her for a while. Inside I was confused; I even asked myself if it was something my brothers or I had done. Had we been too naughty? David always seemed to be getting into fights these days. Had my brother's bad behaviour pushed Dad away? Had Dad suddenly decided he couldn't take any more?

When Dad finally called I was so wound up I could hardly get the words out fast enough. 'Dad where are you? I want to see you. Can I come and live with you? Please!'

I said it so quickly I didn't come up for air.

'I'm at Auntie Chris's,' he said gently. 'It's just for a while, because Mummy and Daddy aren't getting on.'

I had always wanted to think that my parents' relationship was rock solid, but now everything seemed so fragile.

'Please come and get me,' I begged. 'I don't want to be here without you, I want to stay with you.'

'There's just no room, sweetheart. You know how small Auntie Chris's house is.' My dad's voice sounded rough and ragged, but he carried on more firmly. 'Anyway, who would look after you while I was at work? I promise to come and see you at the end of the week.'

While Dad was on the phone my heart was racing, but as soon as the call ended I felt like it fell through the floor. As I replaced the receiver the tears came, and this time there was no holding them back. I felt totally empty, completely alone. Crying silently, I curled up in a ball in the chair he always used to sit in. It was the only place in the house that still felt like home.

That week Dad called me every day, and every night I cried myself to sleep because I missed him so much. I didn't really want to stay with Mum and David, but Dad explained that he just couldn't look after me. Instead, I'd count down the days until I could see him again, either at the weekend or on the odd evening after work. Yet, even in those precious hours, I couldn't talk about how I felt. Dad looked so sad that there was no way I could burden him with more problems.

Without my dad we couldn't afford to stay in the house we were renting, so we moved back to the caravan park and Mum got some work behind the bar. This time our big static caravan was like a small flat, with three bedrooms and a kitchen, a living area, and a little garden around it. Mum seemed to be having a good time with her new park friends, but I was desperately unhappy. The park, which had been the site of so many wonderful holidays, now seemed desperately dreary without Dad around. I was so lonely that I'd spend hours talking to my dolls, pretending they could talk back to me. I'd sent Alice a few letters, and she'd replied a couple of times, but we ended up losing touch. There was no one there to encourage our friendship, and as I wasn't great with my reading and writing, I struggled to keep up with the letters. I felt like I was back to square one: I was all alone, with no friends to confide in.

Life went on like this for almost a whole year, and by the time I turned eleven I had grown used to being lonely. Not wanting to annoy my mum, I had learnt to be more secretive about my unhappiness, although I still found it hard living away from Dad.

Then, word came that Dad had had a really bad accident at work. The blood drained from my mum's face as she took the phone call, but she tried to make light of it to us. It was a shock when I first saw him, though, wrapped in bandages. Dad was left with severe facial injuries and needed looking after, and at first it seemed like the worst thing that could possibly happen. My lovely dad had been seriously hurt and I wasn't even around to look after him. But gradually things actually seemed to get better. Unable to go to work, Dad had a lot of free time to come and see me, and during those visits he and Mum began to talk again. Slowly they rekindled their love for one another. I watched from the background, silently hoping that they would work things out; that my family would be together again. One sunny afternoon they gathered us all together and made an announcement: they were going to give it another try. My brothers just shrugged, but I was over the moon. I couldn't stop smiling and running about the place. Perhaps everything would be all right after all? I was convinced Dad loved Mum so much he couldn't live without her. Now my job, as I saw it, was to make sure that nothing like this ever happened to our family ever again. Mum and Dad were back together, and I was determined to keep it that way, whatever happened. As children too often do, in my head I took sole responsibility for keeping my family happy and together.

As soon as Dad was better, he got a job behind the bar at the caravan park too and so we were settled for a while. However, it wasn't long before Mum and Dad decided that they wanted to try something new and got trained as bar managers. After that life became one long rollercoaster; a rollercoaster with more downs than ups. We moved almost every six months, from one run-down pub to the next, so Mum and Dad could renovate them and turn them into thriving businesses again. While it was good for my parents, it meant I never felt settled anywhere. Most of the time, I didn't go to school – there was so much paperwork involved in enrolling me that, by the time Mum or Dad got round to filling it in, it was time to move again, and so my education really floundered. At the time I didn't realise what problems I was storing up for the future. I just followed my parents wherever they went, relieved that we were all back together again.

It wasn't only my reading and writing that suffered with all the disruption. Moving around so often made it really hard for me to make friends. I'd never been one for chatting easily with strangers and I hated being the new girl, always on the outskirts of the group, always a step behind. It didn't do much for my self-confidence, and I became even more withdrawn and quiet.

I tried to hide my loneliness from Dad; he was so happy himself that I didn't want to spoil things for him. Looking back, it sounds silly, but I was convinced that unless I made it look like we were the perfect family, he'd go away again. Most girls would turn to their mum for comfort if they were unhappy, but I never felt I could do that. Mum just wasn't that kind of mother. It seemed that her priority was her own life now she was running her pubs – being the centre of attention behind the bar – and it felt like she had even less time for me. When I did speak up, it was clear she didn't understand what the problem was.

'David doesn't seem to have any trouble. He's always got friends over,' she'd point out. 'You obviously can't be trying very hard.' While she was speaking, David would make rude gestures behind Mum's back, but she never caught him at it. The conversations would always end with me promising to try harder, and secretly worrying that it was no use.

My friendships with Kate and Alice seemed so long ago that I had forgotten what it felt like to have someone I could confide in. It was about this time that I started comfort eating. There were always crisps and peanuts in the pubs where my parents worked, and I felt less silly sitting on my own in the playground if I had something to eat. It made me feel better while the food was in my mouth, but putting on weight did nothing for my confidence either. My dad always told me I looked beautiful, but I still felt self-conscious, and I ended up spending more and more time by myself.

Although Mum tried her best to be a great parent on a practical level – making sure we were well fed, safe and healthy – she seemed to find it hard to show me any affection. Dad would sit for hours hugging me, but I rarely got a cuddle from Mum. It just wasn't her style. However, I couldn't help noticing she had a lot of time for David. Maybe that's when I first admitted to myself that Mum might love David more than me? Maybe I'd always felt it. Maybe that's why I was always such a daddy's girl?

It was about this time, when I should have been in my last year of primary school, that I realised that David was not the perfect son I'd always thought he was. Mum was so proud that she had a popular, intelligent child that she talked about him all the time. The problem was that the praise went straight to David's head, and I'm sure it made him feel he could do anything he wanted. What he *didn't* want to do was to get on at school.

It wasn't unusual for David to come in after school swinging a letter, and tell my parents: 'Mr Robinson wants to see you in school tomorrow.' Dad would sigh and walk away, but Mum would look panicked and want to know what had happened.

'Oh, David, what have you been up to now?' she'd ask despairingly.

'It's nothing,' he'd shrug.

'Really? Well, why do they want to see me, then?'

'It was just an accident. Nothing serious. But they went mental about it.'

Turns out that this time he was swinging on one of the school doors, and had swung his legs so far up that he kicked a big hole in the ceiling. David sniggered when he told us the story, but the look on Mum's face quickly wiped his smile away.

'And how much will I have to pay for that?' she asked, wearily.

'Dunno. Eighty quid, or something like that.'

'Jesus, David!' But my brother would go and give Mum a hug and she'd forget she was telling him off. Instead she'd try to reason with him and get him to knuckle down and study for his exams.

'I know, Mum. I won't do it again,' he'd assure her, 'but school is so boring . . .'

'But you've got a real gift. A good mind,' Mum would say, trying to make him see straight. 'It's such a waste not to use it.'

David would just shrug his shoulders, not even bothering to argue back.

When Mum read his school reports aloud, it was always the same: David would be top of the class if he didn't waste his natural abilities on winding up his classmates and messing around. Mine were completely different. I'd try and try but still end up at the bottom of the class.

Once I got so frustrated that I actually asked my brother what his problem was.

'David, it's not fair. I hate being dyslexic. It makes everything difficult. You find everything so easy. You could do whatever you want, without even working that hard. So why do you mess around all the time?'

'What've your problems got to do with me? Is it my problem you're messed up in the head?' he'd ask, and walk away, leaving me feeling stupid. No amount of guilt tripping seemed to change David's mind – it was like water off a duck's back.

As I got older I began to learn more about the real David, and the more I found out, the more I worried. Apparently, when he was about three years old, he had had such a temper that he used to hold his breath until he passed out. Mum used to beg him to breathe, but he was so stubborn he'd actually faint. Mum got so worried she took him to the doctors, but there was nothing they could do. 'He'll breathe again once he blacks out. Don't worry, he'll grow out of it,' the doctor reassured her.

David did grow out of holding his breath, but his wilfulness didn't go away. It seemed that wherever there was trouble, David wasn't far behind.

Back when he was nine, for example, and I was too young to realise what was going on, David used to steal from our corner shop. He had a mate called Adam who started nicking things and encouraging David to do the same. Whenever Adam's mum popped in for some milk or bread, the shop owner cornered her and made her settle her wayward son's bill. When David ended up copying Adam, and Mum was similarly presented with a bill, she just grounded him for a few nights and made him do some jobs around the house to pay for it. Mum joked that David could get away with anything when he smiled. She thought he had such an adorable, infectious grin. His chubby little cheeks used to light up a room and so he'd never be in trouble for long. But the lack of discipline meant that nothing was stopping David's behaviour going from bad to worse.

By the time I was eleven, and David was fifteen, I felt that my protective big brother was turning into someone I didn't recognise any more. John Paul was pretty much grown up and living his own life by then, and David and his strange moods seemed very much to rule the roost. What with David's unpredictable behaviour, and Mum and Dad's shaky relationship, our safe, happy family didn't seem so safe and happy any more. However, with no friends and no happy school-life to escape to, I had no choice but to try and keep my family together as best I could.

If I ever spotted David ignoring his chores, he'd come after me and warn me not to tell. 'Hey, Vicky, you didn't see anything then, did you?' he'd snarl, pressing his face so close to mine I felt claustrophobic. 'I was washing up, wasn't I? Don't you go telling on me now, will you? Run along, then.'

It worked – I wouldn't dare tell anyone. The thought of what he'd do if he found out I'd landed him in trouble made me shudder with fear. The glare in his eyes and his eerie, threatening tone of voice were enough to keep me quiet. I had seen for myself how dangerous he could be when he lost his temper, but I still found it hard to believe that this was the same big brother who'd stuck up for me in the playground just a few years ago.

It was around this time that David and a couple of his friends broke into a car that was sitting behind a shop not far from our flat, to listen to the radio. They didn't steal the car, but they sat on the seats, out of the cold, and listened to music. I don't think they bothered to wonder where the owner was. David was always like that. He found it easiest to ignore people who might get in the way of him having a good time. But, eventually, the owner, who was also the shopkeeper, came out and found them. We lived in such a small community – the sort of estate where everyone knew everyone – so he marched David up to our house to tell Mum and Dad. I don't know if it was because my dad was so respected in the area, or maybe because of their young age, but the man decided not to report the boys to the police. Instead he set David and his friends to work, helping him carry boxes. He was moving shops and the lads were at it for four days. At the time is seemed like just another one of David's harmless pranks, but it was getting to the stage when it started to become a shock when David hadn't done anything wrong.

I'm sure that Mum and Dad never thought David's troublemaking would amount to much. I think they assumed it was silly boyish mischief that he'd grow out of. They were wrong. Even I could see that he was just getting worse. Considering how much trouble David got into, Dad was never the shouting type; that was Mum's job. Instead, Dad would take David aside and try and explain to him where he'd gone wrong. David's reaction was normally a blank stare and a shrug of the shoulders – it was hopeless. Even when Mum would shout in frustration, David didn't flinch. Her words kept on falling on deaf ears.

My parents knew he had a side to him that could just suddenly explode, so they decided the best way of dealing with David was to set some house rules, the main one being that he had to be home by 9pm every night. I think they were trying to keep him at home as much as possible, but it just meant that all of David's friends were permanently in his room. I know my parents were just trying to protect David from himself, but what they never realised was that keeping their son on such a short leash could put their daughter in danger.

Back then, David thought a lot of his friends. He spent all of his time with them and, of course, the 9pm curfew didn't stop him getting into trouble in the early evening.

David seemed to have an obsession with cars, and even though he didn't have a driving licence, and no one had actually taught him to drive, he was always keen to get behind the steering wheel of any car and as often as possible. Maybe he liked the idea of being in control, or maybe just the thrill of doing something he wasn't supposed to do? Whatever the reason, he got caught twice in quick succession trying to drive other people's cars. Both times the police came knocking on our door and both times he got off with a warning and slapped wrist. What the police said didn't change anything though. Looking back, I wish we had all taken the police's warning to heart.

By this time, David wasn't just targeting outsiders – he had no scruples when it came to his family either. There were times when David even took Dad's car out for a spin when Dad was busy doing something else. He'd often come back into the house looking shamefaced and holding a steering wheel or a handbrake. 'I only went round the corner. It just came off in my hands,' he would say. Those were the only times I really saw Dad lose his temper, although I think he was more concerned about David hurting himself than his car.

No one liked the fact that David was hanging out with a rough crowd, of course, and messing around with cars. But what really started worrying us all was the increasingly violent aspect of my brother's personality.

David and my oldest brother, John Paul, were like chalk and cheese; their personalities clashed and they were never friends. I couldn't decide whether they just had very different characters and didn't get on, or if it was something much deeper. David used to tease John Paul about his weight and his nose. His nickname was 'Concorde' and John Paul was already very self-conscious about the way he looked. They'd constantly bicker. John Paul was the argumentative one, but it was David who got violent. Their fights and arguments would erupt over the slightest thing – something as petty as John Paul walking into David's room, or someone eating the last packet of crisps, would spark it off. David also never let go of an argument or fight until he had satisfied himself that he'd got his revenge; whether that involved getting Mum or Dad on his side, or hitting John Paul until he was bleeding.

This happened mostly behind closed doors when I was a small child, but shortly after Mum and Dad got back together, I walked in on David and John Paul fighting in David's bedroom. The room had a cream carpet, but by the time they stopped fighting there was bright red blood everywhere. David was hitting John Paul's head against the wall and his nose was bleeding. Mum couldn't even step in, it was that violent – she had to call Dad to come home from work. By the time he got home the place was a mess. Mum tried to clean the blood up but it was useless; there was so much of it that parts of the carpet were stained pink permanently. Even though John Paul was older and bigger than David, David was just so wild and vicious that poor John Paul didn't stand a chance. I remember feeling horrified, screaming at them to stop. That was the first time I realised how violent David could be. From then on I was genuinely scared of him and made an effort to keep out of his way as much as I could. Soon, I barely saw him as my brother. He was intimidating and scary and I found it hard to feel relaxed when he was around.

As I grew up I avoided David more and more. Although he never did anything to me directly, I now knew what he was capable of. For some reason, I was the only one who was never in the firing line. I used to think he left me alone because I was the youngest – the baby of the family. I knew from other families that the bigger siblings looked after the little ones, so I always assumed that's what was happening in our family too. Now I wonder if there was something more sinister going on.

Sometimes, if John Paul shoved me out of the way if I was blocking his path on the stairway or somewhere, David would shout over: 'Leave her alone, will you.' John Paul would shrug and move aside, and I'd be more confused than ever. David would look out for me one minute, but then make me feel scared the next. I never knew what mood he'd be in. He was so unpredictable and would flip so suddenly that I couldn't keep up. I'd wake in the morning and wonder if David would speak to me that day. Or would he push past me and ignore me? He was difficult to understand and so I felt quite apprehensive around him.

There'd be some mornings when we'd be eating our breakfast together and I wouldn't know whether to speak or not, trying to work out what mood my brother was in. 'Someone got your tongue?' he'd joke. That would be my sign he was in a good mood.

'Oh, sorry. I was in a bit of a daze. What are you doing today?'

He'd shrug his shoulders. 'Just hang out, I suppose.'

Even though he didn't have the friendliest of mates, I still longed to be a part of their group some days and join in the fun. He was my big brother and I looked up to him.

'Can I come?' I'd eventually mutter, still a bit cautious of his reaction.

'Vicky, are you joking? You trying to be funny?' he'd sneer, throwing his cutlery into the sink. When he turned around, though, his sarcastic smile didn't match his eyes. 'It's nothing personal. I just don't want you hanging around. I don't know what I might do . . .'

I'd retreat from the kitchen, embarrassed and confused. I'd got him wrong again.

I used to look back and miss the big brother I used to have; the lovely, mischievous child he had once been. I knew Mum missed him even more than I did. She still thought she could reason with him, but more and more people were losing their patience with David. Dad's side of the family had been open about their dislike and mistrust towards him for years. I once overheard my Auntie Chris talking to my parents about it.

'David needs one thing – some strong discipline,' she had said, her arms folded against her chest. I sneaked out of the room but could still hear the raised voices from my bedroom.

'I do try talking to him, you know,' Dad said, sounding annoyed. 'It's no use. We make rules and he just breaks them. We set a curfew and he gets into trouble during the day instead.'

Mum cut in. 'I know he's a bit of a tearaway, but he's only young. He'll grow up and settle down. He's a smart boy. He'll figure out that the way he's acting is stupid.'

'I'll believe that when I see it,' Auntie Chris snorted. 'When are you going to realise that that young man is out of control?'

Secretly I thought she had a point. Mum and Dad had no control over David. He was growing up, but he wasn't calming down. In fact, he kept getting worse.

When David started having girlfriends, at around fifteen years old, he was very open about them. Most boys his age barely introduced their girlfriends to their family but David's girlfriends were always round at our house. He'd talk about every girlfriend like she was 'the one'. Mum knew about all of them. David was never embarrassed or kept them away. He was proud of having a girl on his arm, and despite his unpredictable behaviour, he always seemed to have all these gorgeous girls after him. Even then it was like there was this charming, public David who everyone liked, and then the real, darker David who no one else could see.

I never talked much with David's girlfriends. By now I was keeping out of David's way as often as I could. Even though David was only five years older than me, we were now worlds apart. I used to watch him with his girlfriends and wonder what on earth they saw in him. Partly, I suppose, that was just a normal sibling reaction but David was just so unpleasant that I wondered how he could ever get a girl to go out with him, never mind all these pretty, friendly ones. And once he'd reeled them in, he was permanently nasty to them; it was embarrassing and uncomfortable.

One time, we were all sitting around the dinner table eating our food when David turned round and shouted at his girlfriend.

'Jesus, Julie, can you eat with your mouth closed? You're making me feel sick. I can see all the food in your gob,' he barked.

I felt really sorry for her. She looked absolutely devastated and I could tell she was trying not to cry. I gave her a small smile from across the table but David caught me and glared. I quickly looked down. Julie sniffed, but later on they disappeared up to David's room as usual and shut the door, which was against the house rules. It was like he had cast a spell over her.

That July, much to Mum's dismay, David left school. Julie's parents went away on holiday and David told Mum and Dad her parents had asked him to look after the house while they were away. That was the last we saw of him for about a fortnight – until the police came knocking on the door. Apparently David had had no permission to stay at the house. Julie's parents had, in fact, told her to stay with relatives. Instead, David had stolen a key and they had stayed in the house for a full two weeks, using the car, washing his clothes in their washing machine and cooking meals. In order to play house with his girlfriend David had betrayed everyone's trust. As usual, Julie had done exactly what he told her to do. It was almost like she was more scared of him than she was of anything else.

Julie's parents hadn't suspected a thing until they had spotted the washing machine door was broken and had interrogated Julie until she broke down and confessed. They were so angry that they reported David to the police and forced Julie to finish the relationship. They never saw one another again and, to be honest, I think Julie had a lucky escape. David had to appear in court and was given community service. He'd already been in trouble with the police in the past, but it didn't seem to make any difference. I wondered why the law was so slack on him. If they had taught him a proper lesson, maybe he'd have had to change?

Mum and Dad were frantic with worry about David, but they too seemed unable to do anything about his behaviour. Mum, particularly, seemed to go further into denial the more violent, deceitful and unpredictable her darling son became.

We all hoped, in time, David would change; all of us thought that he couldn't go on like this for ever, that his selfish teenage rebellion would stop and he'd finally grow up. But I, more than anyone else, soon discovered that he was about to get much worse.

4

Fearful

Mum, Dad and I carried on using the caravan park as an escape from day-to-day life as often as we could. But as David grew older and more strange, we all grew further and further apart. He stayed at home at the White Horse pub in Tilbrook a lot more and refused to do anything with the family. He barely spent any time with us, preferring to hang out with his friends and stay with them whenever he could.

I found it hard to pretend to mind this too much. David had begun to make me feel very uneasy. His behaviour became more and more unpredictable and he frequently lost his temper over the slightest thing. One day he made to race straight off after dinner, but Dad stopped him. 'Hold up, David. How about giving your mum a hand with the dishes for once?'

David didn't reply. There was an awkward silence, so Mum cut in: 'Don't worry, love, Vicky doesn't mind helping.'

'No. I think David should do it.' Dad's voice was soft, but firm. David turned on his heels and started shouting in Dad's face.

'Don't you fucking start with me. Don't even fucking start. I didn't even want to eat this muck. Why the fuck should I start slaving after you all?'

Mum shouted 'David!', but he wasn't finished. Towering over Dad and shaking his finger in his face, he hissed at him: 'Who are you to boss me around? Get off my back. I don't have to take this. I don't have to fucking take this any more . . .'

Without even thinking what I was doing, I put my hand on David's arm to calm him down. He grabbed it and wouldn't let me go.

'Get off!' I squealed, and my parents both told him to leave me alone. I thought he might break his rule and hit me then but he just looked at me strangely, laughing cruelly as I tried to squirm away. This was the same brother I used to have play fights with at the campsite, but there was nothing playful about his expression now. As usual, though, Mum then bustled about, making tea and trying to distract her son with chitchat, and eventually David calmed down enough to drop my hand. I legged it for the stairs without looking back. As I sat on my bed, I heard the front door slam and the sound of David's boots as he stormed off to his mate's house, with my dad shouting after him. I could still see the red marks where my brother's hard fingers had gripped me. After that, he was around even less and, to be honest, I much preferred it that way.

The three of us went to the caravan park nearly every weekend and we got friendly with a family who ran the disco during high season. They had a son, Robin, who was eleven like me, and when our parents hung out together so did we. The first time we met he asked me if I'd ever been to his school before, because I looked really familiar. I knew it was just an excuse for him to come and speak to me, but I wasn't used to boys even noticing me. I tried to continue the conversation but I was so shy I couldn't get the words out of my mouth. To start with there were awkward silences and times where we both would be looking towards the floor. 'What have you been doing?' I sometimes managed. 'Nothing much,' he'd say, and then there'd be silence again. And this was how it was for the first few weekends. I fancied him so much I didn't have a clue what to do about it.

Having a crush on anyone was so alien to me. I never liked anyone in school; I always felt so out of my depth. But being so swept away by Robin made me see how much more comfortable I was out of school. Eventually, we hung out so much I stopped being shy. We did all kinds of things together: swimming, chatting and messing about in the playground. I really fancied him, with his baby face and brown, glossy hair. He was funny too and always making me laugh. I'd been having my periods since I was nine years old, so my hormones were all over the place. One look from Robin and I melted. We ended up spending all our time together and we eventually kissed one day while we were walking through the park. It was all pretty innocent, a few kisses behind the hedges is all we managed. I blushed because I fancied him so much, but he was a real gentleman – well, as a girl of my age I thought I was in love and couldn't believe a cute boy like him would fancy a quiet, chubby girl like me. Robin lived on the site so whenever we went back we picked up where we'd left off, but we were just kids messing around and after a few months my first little romance fizzled out.

It seemed that whenever I got close to someone I had to eventually say goodbye, because our family were constantly on the move. Looking back, all the friendships I formed got quickly broken up and I was never able to put roots down anywhere. Although I still loved spending time with Dad, I was getting older and desperate to have someone my own age to be close to and who would always be there.

If I couldn't have a friend I decided the next best thing in the world was a dog, which would always be there with unconditional love and attention. From then on, I never stopped asking Mum and Dad to get me one.

We hadn't lived in Tilbrook village long when I found out there was an RSPCA centre nearby. At any opportunity I'd beg Mum and Dad to take me there to have a look. 'We don't have to bring one home, let's just go and see,' I'd lie. I drove them mad.

Eventually, my parents gave in and we headed for Wood Green Animal Shelter. 'We're only going to have a look,' Mum warned. I was overwhelmed with excitement. As soon as we arrived, I jumped out of the car and ran off. I walked round for ages secretly trying to decide on a dog to take home, but it was impossible to choose because they were all so sweet. Eventually, I spotted one and it was adorable, really mischievous looking. I could see that Mum and Dad were slowly melting. 'Oh, Mum, it's so cute. I promise I'll look after it,' I begged.

'Go on, love,' my Dad put in. 'It'd be company for her when we're with the punters.'

'Mum, I promise I'll walk it every day. And clean it. And brush it . . .'

'OK, enough, enough!' my mum said, putting up her hand. 'I'll go and find out more about it.' When the news came back that the pup had already been found a new owner, I was completely deflated. I couldn't look at any other dog. 'Let's go,' I said, trying not to cry.

I was on my way out, walking past a block of kennels, when a little Collie puppy managed to squeeze through the bars of its pen and fall, tumbling towards me. And that was it: I'd found my best friend – or rather he'd found me.

I picked him up and he licked my fingers. 'Oh, Mum, look! We just have to have this one,' I begged.

Apparently, though, my new soul mate had a bug and the people at the centre weren't sure if they should let him go. I was ecstatic when they eventually decided he'd recover better in the comfort of a family home. I called him Ben and he was by my side from that moment on.

As soon as David found out I'd got a pet, he was jealous. 'I've always wanted a dog too. How come Vicky gets one?' he moaned. Mum tried to get us to share, but I didn't want him going anywhere near Ben. I didn't trust him with anything I loved. So, in the end, Mum said he could have one too. David had always wanted a Doberman – one of his friends had one and he loved it, and I guess he thought it fitted his hard-man image. So, he went to a Doberman rescue centre a few weeks later and brought Taura home, at five-and-a-half-months old. After that, the pub was chaotic. Ben and Taura got on really well, but they were crazy together.

Soon after we got the dogs, it started snowing for months. I remember the pond in the back garden of the pub was always frozen over and the dogs kept slipping on it. Once Taura was chasing Ben so fast she slipped, fell and started whimpering like a baby. I ran into the kitchen to tell David and found him flicking through a car magazine in the kitchen.

'Come quick!' I panted. 'Taura's had an accident!'

'Can't you clear it up yourself? There's a good girl.' He flashed me a smile and turned back to the magazine.

'No, I mean a real accident. She fell over on the ice and I think she might have broken something.'

'I'm sure she's fine, Vicks. She's a tough old bitch.' His voice was totally cold, and he never stopped turning the pages.

'David . . .' His eyes met mine. When I saw the warning look in his eyes, I faltered. 'Don't worry, David. I'll look after her.'

'Good girl!' He leant forward to ruffle my hair. Instinctively I jumped back, but he just laughed and carried on reading.

I stuck to my promise and cared for Taura and Ben all day, every day, because I knew David had no intention of lifting a finger. Taura was a two-minute infatuation that he soon got bored with and cast aside. There were many times she was due her food but he'd go out with his friends instead. I could never watch the dogs go hungry; it'd break my heart seeing them suffer in any way. David, on the other hand, could just ignore it. It was like the suffering of others wasn't even real to him. It sounds silly, but the way my big brother treated the dogs made me shiver. I vowed to protect them, little realising that it was really me who was in danger.

Despite the noisy chaos the dogs brought to the household, it still really bothered me that I didn't have any friends in Tilbrook. Now that I wasn't even seeing Robin any more, there was no one outside of the family I could talk to. Plus, I'd just left the worst school so far – an experience that really scarred me. I was in the first year of a big rough comprehensive, and I hated every minute of it. I'd absolutely dread class, because the letters and numbers would swim across the page, muddling me up and making me want to cry with frustration. To start with, I tried asking for help, but my teacher wasn't sympathetic. One time I was called up to the board while another student explained a grammar point to me. The girl spoke slowly, as if I were an idiot, and the whole class laughed at me

– the stupid new girl. After that it seemed easier to keep quiet and slip further and further behind.

If it was bad in the classroom, the playground was a hundred times worse. I used to walk around on my own, trying to look busy, desperately wishing I had my dogs with me for company. The bullying now was subtler, but just as nasty.

During morning break one of the popular girls came up to sit on the bench next to me. I was thrilled. Usually I just sat and watched the other girls play. Of course, I'd been introduced at the start of the year, but so far everyone had ignored me. I was usually really shy, but by this time I was such a lonely little thing that I smiled at her, and asked if she wanted to share my crisps.

'Vicky . . . It is Vicky, isn't it?' she asked, flicking her long blonde hair. Her name was Amanda, and she looked a bit like my old friend, Alice, I decided.

'Yeah, that's me.' I was so pleased she knew my name that I didn't notice the way her friends were looking at us and sniggering behind my back.

'Well, Vicky, can you keep a secret?' Her eyes were shining and her enthusiasm was infectious, so I nodded my head vigorously. 'Great! Do you know Sam?'

'Yep, I think so.' I tried to play it cool, but everyone knew Sam – he was one of the best-looking guys in our year.

'Well, I reckon he likes you.' Amanda leaned back and crossed her arms, smiling broadly.

'Really?' I couldn't keep the surprise out of my voice. First Robin, and now Sam! 'How do you know?'

She shook the question off. 'Everyone knows. But what are you going to do about it? Want me to talk to him for you?'

'Erm, thanks, but I'm not sure . . .'

'You're right,' she cut in, 'why don't you just speak to him yourself? I'll go with you, if you want.'

I didn't want to let my new friend down, so we strolled arm-in-arm over to the group of boys who were hanging out on the steps. They started laughing as we approached, and I hoped they hadn't been teasing Sam about me. I felt a nervous knot in my stomach, but Amanda squeezed my arm and said brightly: 'Hi guys! Vicky wanted to come and say hello.' They all snickered, but I thought Sam might have blushed a bit. This gave me the confidence to flash him a friendly smile and say: 'Hi, Sam. What are you guys up to?'

I had never been brave enough to talk to the popular lads in school before, but now maybe everything would be different? Maybe now I'd finally fit in?

I was wrong. 'Careful, Sam!' my so-called friend said, putting her arm around Sam's shoulder. 'Vicky's in love with you. She won't stop going on about you. She's got your name scribbled all over her pencil case. She keeps on saying that she wants to marry you and have your babies.'

Sam shrank back from me and all the other guys started wetting themselves with laughter. One guy had been drinking juice from a carton, and he laughed so hard he snorted it out his nose.

'No. That's not . . .! She told me . . .' But no one was listening and I felt utterly humiliated. Before the hot, babyish tears had the chance to fall, I ran off and hid in the toilets, not venturing out until break was over.

The teasing was merciless, and it went on for days. I tried to confide in a teacher, but I was too embarrassed to explain the situation properly, so all I got was a lecture on telling tales. After that I shut up, and eventually the bullies lost interest in me. Shortly afterwards we moved again and

I was reluctant to enrol in a new school and go through it all over again. I thought I'd be happier at home, more confident, safer . . .

By the time I was twelve, and we moved to the pub at Tilbrook, my family and my dogs were my whole world. School didn't get a look-in. When I should have been starting secondary school and making friends my own age, I was helping out in the pub, collecting glasses and serving food, or playing with Ben and Taura in the back garden. School officers got involved, but because we moved so often they weren't very consistent. It was a mess, really. Mum's since told me that she regrets not insisting I attended school because I now struggle with reading as an adult. But there were even darker consequences to my extended truancy. Looking back, I wonder how things might have been if I'd had just one friend in Tilbrook, or one sympathetic teacher. Instead I ended up completely isolated at what was to be the worst time in my entire life.

It was to become the setting for my worst nightmares coming true, but, from the outside, Tilbrook was generally a nice, friendly village. Mum and Dad were well liked, so their friends treated me well too. The pub was not only my home, it also became my social life and day job too. Amongst a group of kids my own age, I'd freeze, get shy and run away. 'So, Vicky, where are you from?' a friendly girl might ask at school. But I couldn't answer. With everyone watching me and waiting for a reply, it always felt like there was too much pressure on me, and instead of answering like a normal person I'd run away. Afterwards I'd hate myself for being so awkward. It sometimes felt like my lips had been sewn shut – a sensation that was to become a horrible part of my everyday reality.

Even back then I was getting used to feeling alone, especially around other kids. From spending so much time with adults, I was more at ease with Mum and Dad's friends, hanging around with the punters when I should've been having fun with other girls my age. And, as I said before, I started my periods early, and by now my body looked like that of a grown woman. So looking back, it sometimes feels like everything was conspiring to make me grow up too fast and rob me of my childhood.

At twelve, with my quick dimples and clouds of dark hair, I was like a mascot for the adults in the pub. Friendly regulars would often chat to me.

'Come and join us, little Vicky,' one of the regulars, Bill, used to say. 'Now, have I told you the story about this place?' I'd shrug, happy to hear the tale again.

'Well, did I ever tell you that this very pub has been a watering hole for centuries? I'm serious. Back in them days, travellers on horseback used to break their journey here. It's got a lot of history, not all of it good, if you know what I mean. Some of it much too horrible for your ears.'

'Give it a rest! Don't you go scaring her . . .' Dad would shout from the bar, but Bill would laugh and continue.

'Anyway, all I'll say is that some folks round here would swear that on gloomy nights they've seen a headless horseman ride through the village.'

'They never!' I'd protest, but Bill was adamant. 'I've seen him a few times myself.'

When the pub was renovated a few years previously the builders had found coffins in the walls, although no one seemed clear whose coffins these were. Locals said that doors would close and open on their own and there was meant to be an old woman who walked around the pub crying for her dead baby. The little hairs on the backs of my arms stood on end as I heard these stories and I clung to my dad's arm. I knew I was being silly; I didn't really believe in ghosts. What I didn't know then, of course, was that there are scarier things than ghosts, and that houses can be haunted by the living as well as by the dead.

Although David and John Paul still officially lived with us, my brothers were back and forth from the pub all the time. Mum never knew where they were. John Paul, who was in his twenties, had his own life to lead. But, still, David would be gone for days sometimes too. I don't know where he called home. He had his own room in the pub, and a lot of his belongings stayed there, but he slept wherever he wanted – if it wasn't a new girlfriend it was one of his mates. He roamed between our home and friends' houses all across the region. He also went back to old villages we'd lived in to see old friends, and then would come back when he'd had enough, or ran out of money. Unlike me, he had no problem making and keeping friends, and despite his violent moods, Mum always kept the door open for him. Whatever he did, he was still her darling little boy.

One week in October, I remember, David had been home for a few days. The atmosphere in the house changed as soon as he walked through the door, like it always did. Everyone seemed to be on pins. I avoided him and whenever he walked into a room I'd walk out again. I just didn't want to take any chances – his moods changed so quickly. At one point he caught my eye as we passed on the stairs and mumbled 'All right?' But I never responded. I knew our relationship was pretty dead. 'Ignore me then,' he'd grumble. It was easier to do just that. If I did talk to him, he'd say something nasty or sarcastic, and I just didn't have the confidence to deal with someone like him.

I was one person David had never physically lashed out at, and I wanted to keep it that way. For someone with so many gifts he was such an angry person, and at seventeen he was so much bigger, stronger and more imposing than me that I just tried to keep out of his way. For some reason that just seemed to wind him up more, and I'd often feel his eyes rest on me with a simmering violence and a strange heat. At the time I assumed that he was thinking about something else: some guy who'd pissed him off or some girl who wasn't falling for his charms. Still, it made me feel uneasy. Even so, there was still a part of me that hoped that one day this frightening man would grow up and change back into the clever, protective brother I had loved so much. That October, when I was twelve, David hung around the pub for days while I kept hoping he'd head off again. I sat by the bar talking to Mum and Dad, like I always did, while my brother stayed in the poolroom with the other lads. 'What are you looking at?' he barked, when he caught me looking across at them.

'Nothing,' I stammered.

'Checking out my mates, are you?' he leered, and they all sniggered.

'No, nothing like that.' My face was bright red. 'Just wondering if you guys were after drinks.'

'Quite the little hostess, ain't she, boys?' For some reason his cronies fell about laughing at that, and I slunk back to the bar.

Even then it seemed so unfair that I was alone, while he was always surrounded by friends and admirers. It was just another thing that made him stronger and me weaker and more vulnerable.

Some days David would sleep all day and wake at night like a vampire, which thankfully meant I barely saw him.

As he wasn't going to school, or working, he could do whatever he pleased. His curtains would sometimes be shut all day and then he'd emerge in the early evening and mess around with his mates. He was a typical older lad, lording it over the younger boys who looked up to him and feared him in equal measures. He and his mates teased the younger kids mercilessly, and David always had to have the final word. In a weird way he was the complete opposite to me: put him in the middle of strangers and he'd start regaling them with some story whereas I'd freeze, unable to get the simplest words out of my mouth. If you've ever had a dream where you've lost all of your teeth, or your mouth has been sewn shut, you'll know what I mean – the feeling that, however much you try, you can't speak up for yourself; that however much you want to it's physically impossible. That was the sensation I was soon to become horribly familiar with, as my waking world turned into a living nightmare.

5

Innocent No More

It was one day that week that my brother put a brutal end to my childhood. When I woke up, I had no idea that this was the day my innocence would be torn away. It started out normally enough, passing without incident until late afternoon. I was sitting in the bar chatting away when I heard Mum shouting from the kitchen. I went running in to see what was going on and spotted Taura munching on a bag of mince off the floor. Mum had left it on the kitchen worktop to defrost for dinner but Taura had jumped up and managed to grab it. I stood there giggling. I thought it was funny, but Mum was furious. 'I wish David would look after his dog better!' she screamed. David stayed in the poolroom, completely oblivious to the chaos in the kitchen, so I helped Mum clean up and prepare another meal for dinner. After a while Mum saw the funny side and we were both giggling together. But in the end it was David who was to have the last laugh.

Later that day I helped Mum tidy the pub ready for the second shift at night – back then pubs were open 11am until 3pm and then 6pm until 11pm – and that evening was like any other. David was in and out of the poolroom. He didn't say a single word to me, didn't even look at me, but there was a kind of manic-ness to the way he was talking and laughing with his mates. He was showing off, the way he did when he'd got out of trouble with the police or got some new girl on his arm. Only vaguely aware of his hyper mood, I chatted to some of the locals. I usually stayed up until about 9pm sitting by the bar, but then I'd say good night to everyone and go upstairs to watch some TV for a while. At about 10pm I went up to my room. It was small, but covered in pictures of animals that I'd torn out of magazines. It seemed very quiet in there after the friendly noise of the pub. I went to bed, and it only took me a few minutes to fall into a deep sleep.

The next thing I remember is waking up because I heard my door opening. I was always a light sleeper – sometimes I'd wake at even a creak in the floor – so it was nothing new. I assumed it was Mum or Dad checking on me. That night I'd been sleeping with my back to the door, so I was just about to turn to see who it was when I felt someone pick up the duvet and climb into bed next to me. I was still sleepy so I wasn't sure what to think. I'd given my dad a quick hug before I went to bed, and it wasn't like Mum to give me a cuddle. Then I heard breathing and I recognised a smell: it was a particular deodorant. I instantly knew it was David. But what was he doing?

Before I could turn around, David started moving his hand down my leg. I froze. Was he going to hurt me? Had I done something to annoy him? But, before anything came to mind or any words left my mouth he yanked on my nightie. It was a pink cotton nightie with frills on the arms and it reached down to my knees. He tugged and tugged until his cold hands were next to my skin. I couldn't move, desperately scared of what he was going to do next.

My mouth opened and I wanted to ask what he was doing but no words came out. I tried to speak, but the words caught in my throat. It was like a nightmare. I opened my mouth to scream but no sound came out. I was petrified. I'd seen what he was capable of but after years of avoiding the wrath of his temper, was I finally going to know what it felt like? Was he going to punish me for something? My entire body was stiff – I must have been like a dead person.

Then I felt something. A hard object was poking my buttocks and next minute the most agonising pain shot up my spine. It felt like I'd been stabbed up my back. I cried into my pillow, but still no words left my mouth. At that point I knew what he was doing – he was raping me. I'd had sex education lessons at school and I knew what sex was. I knew what happened during sex, but I couldn't understand why David was doing it to me. He was my big brother and I knew it was wrong. I felt sick and I was in agony. I'd never felt pain like it. Time seemed to slow down and if I tried to move I felt him move inside me even more. It felt like someone was turning a knife inside me.

David's breathing got faster and faster, his fetid breath hot against my neck. His entire body engulfed mine as his hands wrapped around me, forcing me against him. I wanted to be sick. My body didn't feel like mine. I felt like I was having an out of body experience, watching myself from above. It hurt so much I didn't dare move. I thought moving would make it even more painful so I resolved to stay as still as I could until it was over.

Then, after what felt like hours, but must have been mere minutes, it stopped. David's breathing slowed down and I felt him pull away. He slipped out from under my duvet and, even though I was relieved that the pain had stopped, I was terror-struck, wondering if he was going to do anything else. I didn't move for ages. I didn't even want to turn round in case I faced him. I waited until I heard him leave and close the door behind him before I broke down. I sobbed and sobbed into my pillow. I ached down below, but I pulled my legs up to my chest and curled into a ball, crying my eyes out. I felt so confused. I pulled my nightie back over my legs and cried and cried. The physical pain had now subsided but it was replaced by emotional and mental pain. My head felt like someone had just told me the most horrific story and I couldn't let it go.

I lay in bed in exactly the same position for hours, scared he'd come back or do something else, something even worse. I was totally confused – I kept asking myself over and over again what it had meant. It didn't feel real. Had I done something to make him think I wanted him to do that? Does he fancy me? I knew what it was like to have a crush, but having my own brother think of me that way was too much to understand. As far as I was concerned that sort of thing didn't happen. I was very well developed, had breasts and looked a lot older than my years, but, still, my brother wasn't meant to do those kinds of things to me. I just couldn't understand how it happened. So I started wondering if he was punishing me for something? Was I spending too much time with Taura? Had I eaten his share of food at dinnertime? Did I get more attention from Mum and Dad? All kinds of ideas spun around in my head, but none of them made any sense. I wanted to run to the bathroom and be sick, to get rid of the badness inside of me and release the knot in my stomach, but I was too scared to leave my room.

Eventually, I managed to uncurl my body and get up, but still I couldn't leave my room. I pushed the bed up against the door instead. At least that way he wouldn't be able to come back in. A few hours later, I heard Mum and Dad go to bed. I heard their footsteps pass my room. As far as they were concerned they had closed the pub like any other normal night, completely unaware that their daughter's world had just been turned upside down. I was so tempted to shout for them, to be comforted by them and have them protect me, but something stopped me. I don't know what or why, but I couldn't imagine the words leaving my mouth. It felt so alien. Nothing in my life had prepared me for something like this to happen. I just couldn't take it in. I didn't even believe what had actually happened to me, so how could I begin to tell anyone else? It seemed so unreal; I just couldn't believe my big brother had done that to me. How would Mum and Dad react? Would Mum believe me? If I told Dad, he'd want to hurt David; he'd want to kill him. What then? Would Dad go to jail because of me? Would I be taken away from my parents? Although my body had been used like an adult's body, I still thought like a child, and I was utterly confused.

Mum and Dad had not long got back together and, up until tonight, my world had finally seemed safe and secure again. I was petrified that telling Mum and Dad the truth about the monster their son had become would break them up again, and I couldn't bear the idea of being responsible for destroying my family. I wanted everything to go back to how it was before. I was just a scared little girl. My world had been torn apart and I had no idea how to put it back together.

So many contradictory thoughts ran through my mind. In the end, I heard my parents' door shut and them switching their light off. My chance had gone, and I sobbed silently all that long night, terrified that David would return.

6

Disgusted and Defenceless

When I woke up the next morning, I was back in my old life for a wonderful few seconds before the memories of the horrors of the night before hit me. 'Did I dream it all?' I wondered for a moment, hoping against hope, but then I moved and an aching pain emerged between my legs. It brought me back down to earth with a bang. But although the pain was very real, it just didn't seem believable that David could have raped me. How could my brother do something like that? I didn't want it to be real. 'It just couldn't have happened' I said over and over in my head, trying to convince myself.

I was desperate to go to the toilet but I was frozen with terror. 'What if I pass him on the landing?' I thought. 'He might do it again. He's capable of anything.'

Eventually I had to go as I couldn't keep it in any longer, so I cautiously moved the bed away from the door, peered through the crack, and then ran across the small space between my bedroom and the bathroom. Locking the door firmly behind me, I looked at my reflection in the mirror but I didn't recognise the girl with the puffy eyes looking back at me. What did I do? Why does he hate me that much? Has he done it to other girls? I had so many unanswerable questions floating around in my head. Questions no girl my age should have to ask. I was surrounded by reminders of our everyday family life – Dad's razor on the side of the bath, Mum's dressing gown on the back of the door, David's toothbrush nestling against mine in the holder. I couldn't believe that everything looked so normal, so innocent, when my whole life had been destroyed overnight.

Relieving myself was painful; it stung terribly. I carefully washed between my legs and then tried to bring my face back to normal by splashing it with cold water. Again, I had to brave myself for the short journey across the landing but I knew I couldn't stay in the bright, reassuring light of the bathroom forever, so I ran back to my bedroom and got changed. I felt better with my clothes on, more protected, and I sat on my bed for a few minutes trying to pluck up the courage to go downstairs. The thought of seeing David at the breakfast table was making me feel sick.

'What do I do?' The question ran over and over in my head until I felt sick and giddy. 'What do I do?'

Even though I was close to Dad and had always felt like I could tell him anything, I knew if I told him what had happened to me it would break him. I knew that he'd feel somehow responsible, like he hadn't protected me properly. I just couldn't do that to him, especially now he was so happy with Mum. I was so scared that he would somehow love me less. Would he think I was to blame? Would he see me differently? I loved being his little girl and thought he would be disgusted by me if he knew what my brother had done to me.

I also worried about whether Mum would even believe me. Mum thought so much of David; would she believe he could do such a thing? He was often in and out of trouble, but this was a completely different thing. Would she believe that her precious son had raped her daughter? And if Mum didn't believe me, would Dad take her side?

All kinds of thoughts were spinning around in my head. It somehow felt easier to hide and pretend it had never happened. In a way, I felt like I was protecting my parents from themselves – it would be easier on them if I didn't tell. I loved them fiercely; this would ruin everything and turn our family upside down. I didn't have a single friend outside of the family; there was no one else who cared for me. Even though my life had been ruined, I couldn't bear to feel responsible for ruining everyone else's by telling. I was just twelve years old and I simply couldn't take in what had happened.

I was still sat on my bed when Mum called out to me.

'Vicky, are you up? These dogs need feeding,' she shouted up the stairs. I jumped out of my skin, like someone had just violently shaken me out of a dream. My head was full of so many questions and emotions that I couldn't think straight.

'Get a grip Vicky,' I told myself, and I got on to my feet. I took a deep breath and walked down the stairs. My legs were so weak I thought I might collapse, and still I could feel the nausea rising in my throat, ready to burst out as soon as I opened my mouth. My stomach felt like it had hundreds of butterflies flying around inside.

'I have to tell Mum and Dad,' I kept thinking. I tried thinking of a sentence, a word, anything, just to get their attention. But my mind was in a state. I couldn't think straight for one second. All kinds of thoughts were overtaking one another and inside I was screaming in confusion.

I turned the corner without realising and before I knew it I was standing in the kitchen.

'Oh, there you are,' Mum laughed. 'Look at these dogs, they're starving!' She was smiling, bustling around like nothing was wrong. I'd never felt my heart beat so fast and heavy in all my life. I thought I was going to collapse. I imagined I looked a state, white and sweaty and scared, but Mum obviously didn't notice anything odd about my appearance.

'Please, ask me what's wrong!' I begged inside. I was desperate for her to ask me, anything to help me get the words out. I didn't feel strong enough to say it myself, to form the words: 'David raped me'. If only I had someone to weave it out of me – if only. I hovered on the spot for a few seconds, trying to put one foot in front of the other, but feeling frozen to the floor.

'C'mon Vicky, we haven't got all day. There's lots to do today,' Mum added, before walking out of the door. I managed a thin, wavering smile and then the moment was gone, and I was lost. I felt numb. I went over to the dogs' bowls, looking around the room hesitantly – thankfully no one was there. No sign of David. I let out a huge sigh of relief. I gave Ben a big hug, feeling reassured as he licked my face, and then I let him and Taura out while I prepared their food. I kept looking over my shoulder waiting for David to appear. Where was he? I was desperate to find out but I didn't want to ask Mum in case I broke down and gave myself away. I kept waiting for the right moment to tell her. I didn't manage to eat any food that morning; I couldn't even stomach a drink. Everyone was busy and getting on with their day. If only they knew what had happened to me last night. Even if I had wanted to tell them, how could I? When? They had no time to sit down with me and talk and I didn't have the words.

I hadn't been going to school for months, but for the first time in ages I wondered if it would be a better place to be than my home that morning. Ignored and cast aside at school, or this horrifying new world of fear and intimidation at home? It was too much to get my head around. What had I done to deserve all this? I cried inside. I wanted to curl up and sleep and never wake up; this was too tough and adult for a shy, scared child like me to deal with.

But as much as school might have been an escape for other girls, for me it wasn't really an option. I didn't think I could cope with the bullying on top of everything else. Someone would say something mean and, in that state, I would have just fallen apart, spilling my poisonous secret everywhere. It wasn't like there was a friend or teacher who I could ask for help or advice. I had no choice but to stay where I was.

I clung to Mum and Dad, following them round like a shadow to avoid any danger of being alone. I didn't see David all morning and the tension was unbearable. Every nerve in my body was straining to listen out for his heavy footsteps, the smell of his deodorant.

A few hours later, I was in the bar with Mum.

'Do me a favour, sweetheart,' she said. 'Can you polish the brass for me again? Thanks, petal.'

I didn't utter a word, just got on with the jobs like I always did. I walked around like a ghost. I'd never felt so dead and confused in all my life. I felt empty inside, like someone had ripped out my feelings and emotions. Every time I turned a corner I held my breath, wondering if I'd see David.

And then, just after lunch when I was sitting at the bar drinking, he came in. I couldn't look up. I just heard his voice, saying something to the boys around the bar, and then I felt his eyes burning into my skin. And then he went straight into the poolroom without speaking to me, without touching me. He acted like nothing had happened.

I couldn't believe it. It made me hope again that it had been a dream, praying it wasn't true. There was no way he could be so casual about attacking me, was there? I desperately wanted to believe it was all just a horrible nightmare. But then I caught a waft of his deodorant again, and I knew that it was all too real.

I couldn't breathe. I'd suffered with asthma from a young age and I pulled out my inhaler, but my mouth went dry, my hands turned clammy and my heart beat faster than it had ever done before. I started swinging my legs and bouncing on my stool – I just couldn't keep still. It was like my body was doing whatever it had to in order to cope. I looked up towards Mum and Dad. Should I tell them? Should I do it right now? I asked myself. But they were chatting away with friends, laughing with big grins on their faces. What would I say? In a way, I suppose I wanted them to notice that something was wrong with me, that I was unusually quiet, so they could ask me something. That would give me an opportunity to tell them and it'd be easier. But they didn't notice a thing; they were too busy with the bar to notice anything about me. I couldn't bear the idea of destroying their world. They'd hate me, turn against me, and I'd be completely alone. In the end I decided it was just easier on everyone to keep quiet.

For the rest of the day I walked around the pub, following Mum and Dad like a lost puppy, half asleep. Trying to force my mind away from the terrors of the night before, I focused on helping my parents get the bar ready. I polished the warm mahogany until it glowed and wiped down the brass labels of the beer. Even the sour smell of the empty spills trays was a welcome distraction from my whirling thoughts. How could I be in danger here? I was surrounded by objects as familiar as old friends. In my dazed state, the comforting bulk of the cigarette machine seemed as good a protection as any other. But then, as soon as I'd convinced myself I was safe, David would stride across the pub's threshold without a care in the world and I'd be plunged back into the new, brutal world he'd made for me.

I avoided his eyes like a frightened animal, but it didn't help. It was like I knew he was there without looking up and I felt like I was going to self-combust until he'd leave again. When my parents were busy I'd feel him stare at me so hard that I worried he would leave a mark on my skin. I couldn't bear to think about what he might have been thinking. I felt dirty and disgusting. Still, no one noticed. All I could think about was why? My mind was whirling. I went through almost every day of the last year but still no answers came to mind. I wondered if someone had said something about me; had John Paul been winding him up about being soft with me? I racked my brain, going over every possible reason why he could have wanted to hurt me so badly.

As the sun went lower and lower in the sky I became more and more panicky. If only it could have stayed day for ever, I could have coped with it, I could have stayed strong. But no one heard my silent prayers, and far, far too quickly it started getting dark.

That night I went to bed as late as I possibly could. I kept finding little jobs to do around the bar, making myself useful to put off the moment when I had to leave the safety of my parents.

'Vicky, it's late, go on up,' Mum ordered, when I was still downstairs at 10pm. I stood, just looking at her, searching for the words to tell her how terrified I was of going to bed. But what could I say? She'd already turned to serve a customer and so, with a heart of stone, I climbed the stairs up to my bedroom. Looking back, it was like I was climbing the steps of a scaffold, trudging towards my own downfall.

I climbed into bed and I lay still, petrified. I was scared of going to sleep but I was totally exhausted. The emotional strain of the day had taken its toll so, although I fought sleep for as long as I could, my body betrayed me and I dropped off. I must've just closed my eyes when I heard a noise. The door creaked and the landing light shone into the room. This time I knew what was coming. I wanted to scream but I couldn't get any sounds out of my mouth.

I smelt David's odour as he climbed in my bed behind me. I held on to my nightie and tried to wrap it around my legs, but I was scared that if I resisted too much he'd hurt me even more. He tugged on my nightie again. I tried to hold it tight between my legs but his tugs got harder until eventually his hands were on my skin again. I didn't know what to do. Knowing what was to come, should I get up and run or wait until it was over? If I stayed still, was I allowing him to rape me? But, if I run, would he catch me and hurt me even more? Would he kill me? All sorts of thoughts were running through my head. But, before I could decide what to do for the best, I felt his arms wrap around me and pull me close to him. He raped me from behind all over again. His hands pulled me hard into him. The pain was excruciating. I felt so sick. I could hear him panting and his body was hot and clammy next to my bottom. It felt so disgustingly wrong, but I was so trapped and fearful of what he'd do. Tears filled my eyes and rolled silently down my cheeks, forming a wet patch on my pillow. I kept my body stiff, hoping it'd ease the pain, but it didn't. I looked at the pictures on my wall, stared out my window, anything to help me deal with the pain. Minutes later it was over and he shuffled out from under the duvet. My brother didn't utter a word, and then he was gone, just like that. He closed the door behind him and I cried and cried. David was like a ghost in the night, flying into my room, taking what he wanted and leaving without saying a word. Why was he doing this to me?

I barely slept all night and when the sun shone through my curtains in the morning I went to the bathroom and lay in a hot bath. I scrubbed and washed myself hard to try and remove the dirt I felt creeping all over my skin. I felt like my entire body was crying on the inside. The tears falling didn't make the pain any easier, so what use was it to cry? I longed to be the innocent girl I had been a few days ago. Even though life hadn't been a bunch of roses, it was still better than feeling the way I did now. I felt like I was living in hell.

David was gone by the time I went downstairs a few hours later. Thankfully he'd gone off with his mates so I didn't have to see him yet. As I walked into the lounge I couldn't even look Mum or Dad in the eye.

'Morning love,' Mum sang. I was so disgusted with myself I couldn't look up. 'Are you OK?' she added. I stood still staring at the floor for a moment. 'Vicky? Everything OK?' she asked again, but as I tried opening my mouth the words wouldn't come out. A few seconds passed and I just stood frozen to the spot. 'Oh, stop playing games with me, Vicky. On your way,' Mum spat the words out, clearly annoyed by my strange behaviour.

I felt so dirty. This was even worse than yesterday. I hated myself even more because I wasn't able to stop David abusing me, and so, in a way, I felt like I was making it happen, or at least allowing it to happen. Mum left the room and I looked around; everything looked so different. Even the television and sofa looked different, because my life had changed so drastically. Nothing would ever be the same. I sat on the sofa for a while but it felt uncomfortable, after what David had done to me. My life as I knew it was gone for ever – just curling up on the sofa felt unnatural and disgusting. I tried to remember my life, the state of my mind and body two days earlier but I couldn't focus and everything was a blur. All I could feel was pain and disgust. My whole being was ravaged with fear, and happiness was a distant memory.

I did my duties as best I could without showing I was in discomfort down below, and then I escaped outside. I sobbed as I hugged Ben in the garden. I took him for a long walk so I could be alone. 'Is this going to go on every night?' I thought. 'How can I stop him? What can I do?' I was so angry with myself for letting it happen. Looking back, it makes me so sad that instead of being angry with David, I started hating myself for being so weak and vulnerable. If felt like there was no one I could trust, no one I could turn to for protection. I couldn't even bear to imagine the look on my Dad's face when he realised what a terrible thing had been done to his little girl. No, on some level I felt like it was my own fault that David had hurt me like this, and I would have to deal with it myself.

I didn't see David all day. Mum didn't even mention him. It was like I had wished him away. If only that had been true . . . If only that could have been the end of my ordeal.

The day flew past. I kept checking the clocks, seeing how long I had to come up with a way of fighting him off. But I was so traumatised that it was all I could do to sleepwalk through the day. Before I could even think clearly it was evening and I was sent back up to that little room. My stomach churned with hot dread.

That night I went to bed and chose a longer nightie from my drawer, an old-fashioned one that fastened high up my neck and reached right down to my ankles. I didn't own any pyjamas and going to bed in your clothes was unheard of. In my little twelve-year-old mind the only way of protecting myself was to find a better nightie, one that would cover my body. I lay in bed and waited. I had to stay awake. I had to come up with a plan to stop him. But again my eyes flickered; the tiredness of two sleepless nights mixed with two days of being completely emotionally drained had wiped me out. I was exhausted. I don't know what time it was but I heard a creaking sound echo through the room, sounding alarm bells in my head. How I wished it were Mum or Dad checking up on me, tucking me in for the night. But deep down I knew it wasn't. I knew he'd come back.

With my back to the door again I couldn't see anything and I kept my eyes closed, hoping it'd make things easier, less real. The next minute I felt the duvet move and I smelt David's familiar smell. It made me want to throw up and my whole body started shivering. I kept my eyes shut this time, sealing them closed like I was trying desperately to avoid seeing a ghost. I tried to imagine anything but David's face but, as David pulled my body from behind towards him again, it was hard to imagine anything when the stabbing, sickening pain started all over again. As he raped me, a constant knifing agony shot through my body. I don't know how I managed not to scream. The pain was as bad as the first and second time, almost unbearable. But I knew it was only going to last minutes so I held on, trying to think of something else. Anything to block my thoughts. It was exactly the same nightmarish experience as before: the thrusts, the grunting, and the clamminess. It was also every bit as disgusting as the other times – worse, because I was more aware of what was happening. My brother didn't utter a word. It was like he'd sneaked into a shop, pinched what he wanted and sneaked back out again. Within minutes it was over again and he was gone.

I lay in my bed overcome with anger and disgust. I wanted to scream at the top of my voice, but I clamped my hand over my mouth. The smallest sound might bring him back and then what would happen? Would he rape me again? Would he kill me? Would he hurt my parents? My brother had broken every taboo by forcing himself upon me – there was literally nothing he wouldn't do to get what he wanted.

David had such a humiliating hold over me, but I was so desperate to be free of him. I started to toss and turn with frustration. It was unbearable. 'What am I going to do?' I thought. 'What if it goes on for ever? I can't stand it; I'll die if it happens again. I'll have to run away,' I concluded, hugging myself tightly. Even with so many emotions running through my veins, I still didn't cry. The tears were somehow blocked, just as my voice had been and anyway, what good would crying do? Everything felt so useless. If only I could turn to someone. If only I could trust Mum to support me. Even if she did believe me, how could I do that to my dad? Would he go after David? Would David hurt him back? I was terrified of the outcome. Could I really let my whole family be torn apart? Whatever I did, I'd have to live with the consequences for life. The more I thought about telling, the more impossible it seemed. How on earth would people cope? It seemed so incomprehensible.

* * *

The next morning I had another bath, but this time, instead of fighting back tears, I was angry. I was consumed with rage that I was letting David rape me. I took Ben and Taura for another long walk afterwards – it was my only chance to be on my own with my thoughts. As I walked I got angrier and angrier. Instead of asking questions that were never going to be answered – Why was he doing this? What had I done wrong? – I started thinking about ways I could stop him. The easiest way would be to tell someone, but what if he persuaded everyone that I was lying? How could I argue with him? I didn't feel strong enough. I didn't have faith in the people around me to save me. Even at twelve years old, I knew it was useless to rely on others. The only person who had ever stood up for me was now my biggest enemy. I was totally alone. 'I have to do something myself,' I thought. I spent the day thinking of different options – could I ask for a lock on my door? Maybe I could move the chest of drawers up against the door? Anything to keep that monster out.

When I got home late that afternoon, I heard Mum and David having problems with the bathroom door. As I went up to my bedroom I could hear them trying to get into the bathroom. No one was inside, but the door was locked and they just couldn't get in there. Then, suddenly, the door just opened. 'Oh my God!' I heard Mum laugh. 'It must be the ghost everyone talks about.' It freaked everyone out.

Normally I would've joined in the laughter, but now I had no enthusiasm for anything. I'd never been scared of ghosts, but now I had far scarier thoughts going through my head. Ghosts were nothing compared to the real-life horrors that haunted my nights.

As I sat on my bed listening to their shrieks of laughter, my thoughts were spinning madly. Part of me was listening

Silenced

to what was happening outside my room, while another part of me was obsessively thinking over the past week. Right then and there I suddenly thought of a plan to avoid David at bedtime. The ghosts were a perfect excuse. I could use them as a reason why I never wanted to be alone.

That night, I was about to go up to bed when I cornered Mum.

'I don't want to sleep alone tonight,' I said. 'What if the ghosts lock me in my bedroom like they locked the bathroom door today?' My heart was hammering in my chest, and I must have looked petrified, but that was all part of the plan.

'Oh, don't be silly, Vicky, your bedroom is fine,' she tried to reassure me. But this time I wasn't going to be cast aside.

'No, Mum, I can't,' I announced, my voice trembling, 'I'm going to sleep in your room.' With that I turned on my heels and walked away, praying she wouldn't come after me and tell me she wasn't having any of it. She must have noticed how white I was because she didn't argue anymore. When I was safely round the corner, I slumped against the wall in relief. I was safe. For tonight, I was safe.

That night I curled up on Mum and Dad's sheep rug at the bottom of their bed. Part of me knew my brother would never get me here, but I also worried about my little safety net. It seemed such a flimsy solution. David had proved he was capable of anything. Eventually I managed to sleep and, even though I awoke randomly throughout the night, I was left alone in my warm, furry rug. I was so relieved I wanted to cry.

When Mum and Dad woke up the next morning and found I was still there, they thought I was crazy. But being thought crazy was the last thing I had to worry about.

'It's those ghosts,' I claimed. 'They freak me out.'

'Vicky, you're a big girl,' my mum said, sighing. 'Why are you acting like such a baby?'

'Hey now, it doesn't matter, does it?' my dad would ask her, then turn to me. 'Don't fret, sweetheart. No need to be scared of ghosts. They won't dare come near you when your scary old dad is around.'

I managed a watery smile at the sight of my skinny dad flexing his muscles, relieved that they didn't suspect a thing. After that I said it every night. Some nights Mum lost her patience and told me not to be stupid, so I got cleverer and watched TV until late, waiting until Mum and Dad went to bed too before curling up on their rug without them knowing. Fear made me resourceful. They thought I was mad, but I stuck to my ghost story so, in the end, they didn't make an issue of it any more.

I'll never know if David went into my room looking for me. Even the thought of his step on the floorboards sent shivers down my spine and I suffered through many sleepless nights, convinced that he'd find a way to get to me. If my own bedroom wasn't safe, how could anywhere be? All I know was that he didn't find me in my new hiding place and for that I was so unbelievably relieved.

For the next few weeks I spent every night in Mum and Dad's room, and every waking minute trying to stay away from David. It was a matter of life and death for me to avoid him and I treated it like it was a military operation. Weeks passed without me seeing any more than his shadow, or hearing any more than the muffled echo of his voice from the poolroom. But, after about a month, I walked into the kitchen one day and there he was, preparing some food on the worktop. I saw the back of him and, as quickly as I spotted him, I walked back out again. Afterwards, I locked myself in the bathroom and tried to stop shaking. He had been close enough to touch me. I tried to make sure that would never happen again. Thankfully, because of his nomadic nature – David was always moving around and visiting friends – it was possible to stay clear of him. Mum and Dad didn't suspect anything. They just thought we acted like typical siblings, fighting more as we became teenagers. If only they had known how twisted our relationship had really become.

As the weeks passed I began to believe that David enjoyed coming home and terrifying me, keeping me on edge.

One morning I came out of the kitchen with a packet of crisps in my hand. I was about to open them and tuck in when David appeared from nowhere and headed straight for me. Instinctively, I spread myself across the hallway wall. If I could have had one wish at that moment it would have been to be able to walk through walls and escape from him. I wanted to close my eyes and pretend I couldn't see him. In the end, his strides slowed down, just like everything became slow motion except my racing pulse and tangled thoughts. With my heart beating so fast it felt like it was going to explode, my head spinning and my hands so sweaty I could barely grasp my packet of crisps. But David walked by. He had a spiteful smirk on his face that was so eerie it could've scared a ghost. I looked to the floor as I felt him brush past me. The touch of his body made my skin crawl. Thankfully, he didn't say a word. I couldn't even look up. He walked by and didn't do a thing. It was enough to leave me a shaking wreck.

Some mornings, when David was home, I waited for him to use the bathroom and leave the house before I even got out of bed. It was easier, as that way I knew there was no chance of bumping into him. Other times I somehow made sure I was always with someone if he was around. I was living with a man I hated, and my biggest fear was that he'd try to get me alone. The very thought made me sick with terror.

I silently rejoiced when David was away with friends for days on end. It was such a relief not having to walk around and live every day in his shadow. Those days I relaxed a little, but I still couldn't forget what had happened. Even when his presence wasn't a constant reminder, it was impossible to forget. I hoped it'd be a case of out of sight, out of mind. But, as soon as his name was spoken, my body tensed up, as if it remembered what he'd done to it. If I was sitting at the bar and Mum mentioned his name, I'd spin round on my stool and look to the door fearing he'd come into the room. When he was home, I was always watching and waiting before I did anything to make sure our paths didn't cross. It was stressful and I was constantly on edge. My brother only had to shout from one room and Mum answer him, and my heartbeat would gallop out of control, my asthma would come back and breathing would be hard. Mum thought it was just my asthma getting worse but I soon started to realise that it wasn't just asthma – it was full-blown panic attacks. Looking back, even my body was crying out for help.

In those nightmarish first weeks there were many times when I wondered if I wanted to go on and if I could handle living like this for ever. But whenever I thought about suicide, I drew back from the prospect. How could I do that to my parents? How could I let him win? But every part of every option was terrifying to me. Despite the bustle of the pub I was totally alone, and had no idea which way to turn.

Amongst my dark depression, I managed to hold on to a tiny glimmer of hope. I tried to tell myself that what had happened was a horrible, devastating thing, but at least it was now over. Now I knew what David was really like, I could stay out of his way and stay safe. I'd managed to stop him raping me, and I tried to convince myself to just get on with things. I was determined that no one had to know anything about it. No one else would have to be hurt by his loathsome actions. It could just be my painful secret. If I didn't tell them, no one would ever know. But, in that, as in so many things, I was so very, very wrong.

7

Safe and Sound

One morning, a few weeks later, I woke up feeling incredibly sick. I lay on the warm, comfortable sheep's wool rug at the bottom of Mum and Dad's bed hoping it'd pass, but it just got worse. Next minute I ran straight to the bathroom and threw up.

'Oh, sweetheart, are you OK?' Mum asked, fetching me a glass of water.

I nodded mutely, kneeling on the bathroom floor.

I assumed I'd just eaten something dodgy, and spent the day snuggled up on the sofa with Ben, but I ended up being sick every day that week.

'We need to take you to the doctors, don't we?' Mum said, when it became obvious this was no ordinary bug.

'All right, Mum,' I said, pleased to have her attention, and little thinking what the real cause of my sickness might be.

A few days later, I had an appointment with the doctor. I'd only been there a few minutes when he looked me up and down and diagnosed an infection. He gave me some antibiotics and sent Mum and me on our way. I took the pills for a week, trusting the doctor to make me better, but nothing changed. Mum couldn't understand why I was still sick every day and she started to get really frustrated. I wasn't dwelling on it as much as she was though; I suppose

I just assumed Mum would sort me out. So, we went back to the doctors again and, after glancing at my notes, the doctor motioned for us to sit down.

'Now, Vicky, I hope you don't mind me asking, but have you started your periods?'

I glanced across at Mum. 'Yes, I started them ages ago.'

'And what was the date of your last period?'

I wracked my brains. 'Erm, I think I might have missed the last few,' To be honest, what with everything that had happened to me, my irregular periods seemed the least of my worries.

'That'll be the virus interfering,' Mum said. 'She's been ill for weeks now. No wonder her body is a bit messed up.'

'Not to worry. We'll just run a few more tests and see if we can find out what the problem is.'

'Well, yes, that would be useful,' Mum said, tightly.

As we left I smiled at the doctor, but I could see that Mum was getting more and more irritated with the situation.

A few weeks later, Mum and Dad were reassigned to another pub down the road and we moved to the White Lion, in Bloxham. David had just moved in with his new girlfriend, Lol, so thankfully he was spending less and less time with us. But that week he came to help, and his menacing presence seemed to turn my stomach even more than ever. As we packed up all our belongings, I had to keep running off to the toilet to be sick.

In a way it was a good distraction for me; I was worrying more about my illness than I was about David. And he couldn't stand sick people, so he kept out of my way. By now I was ill so much of the time that I wasn't even getting as upset as I normally did about a move. I liked Tilbrook village, of course, but after everything that had happened there it was a relief to be moving on. The bedroom that I used to love and had spent ages decorating with cut-out magazine pictures of animals was filled with horrible memories. Every time I had to go back in there to change my clothes, my breathing would become laboured and I'd have to force myself not to run out into the hallway. Every time the lights went off at night I kept imagining that I'd heard the floorboards creak in the hallway. Maybe in a new place I wouldn't be so haunted by what my brother had done to me?

Bloxham was just a few miles down the road, but to me it was a fresh start. My sickness was still bad and my legs had started to ache so as soon as we unpacked, Mum quickly registered with a new GP and my records were sent over.

When I eventually got an appointment with the new doctor, Mum was at her wits' end. She was desperate for this new doctor to find out what was wrong with me, and by now so was I.

'I'm sorry, doctor, but this has been going on for weeks now,' Mum complained. 'We need to find out what's wrong with her.'

'Yes, yes, of course. I understand.' This doctor had a very reassuring voice. I tried to convince myself that he'd make me better. After looking carefully at me and my mum, he did more blood tests and felt my glands, my pulse and my spine.

'Hmmm . . .' he said, rubbing his chin. I leant forward, worried about what he was going to say, but it was Mum he spoke to, not me.

'I think your daughter must have a calcium deficiency. That'll be what is interfering with her periods.' I sat up, relieved. After all that, it didn't sound very serious.

'Are you sure that's all it is? Are you sure?' my mum asked, looking hard at him.

'Yes, well, that seems the most probable cause of her symptoms. I'll print you off a prescription and she'll soon be feeling lots better.'

Mum took the prescription without a word, grabbed my hand and then stormed out.

On our way home Mum was quiet for ages, which was not like her. I was just trying to figure out why she was behaving so strangely when she stopped, turned to me, looked me straight in the eye and asked: 'Vicky, could you be pregnant?'

I almost swallowed my tongue in shock. 'No, don't be stupid,' I stammered, but even as the words left my mouth my mind started whirling.

'Sorry. Sorry, love.' My mum looked so relieved. She gave me a quick hug, and an apologetic smile, and we carried on walking.

From that moment on, I couldn't get the idea out of my head. What if she's right? What if I *am* pregnant? My periods had been regular since I'd started at nine years old, and I knew how pregnancy interfered with periods. So was this the answer? Was this why I'd been so ill? It was a terrifying, sickening thought. What if I was pregnant with my brother's baby? How would I explain it to people? They'd never understand. What could I say? No. It couldn't be true. There was no way! I became more and more agitated at the thought of it until I couldn't breathe. Wordlessly, my mum passed me my inhaler. She didn't look so relieved any more.

Later that afternoon, I was lying on the sofa getting some rest and trying to stop my head whirling when

David's girlfriend, Lol, came in. I liked Lol – I thought she was sweet, and couldn't imagine what she was doing with David. I wanted to warn her off him, but whenever I tried she just laughed and put it down to sibling rivalry.

'How are you, hon?' Lol asked, sitting next to me on the sofa.

'Better, I think.' I said, carefully.

'Good, good.' She paused, looking at me. 'Now, don't take this the wrong way, Vicks, but your mum thinks you might be pregnant. Is there anything you want to tell me?'

I couldn't believe it: David's new girlfriend was asking me if there was anything I wanted to tell her. 'Yeah, if only you knew!' I thought, bitterly, but deep down I knew she'd never believe me. Instead, I stared at her blankly.

'No, I'm OK, thanks. Mum is just worrying. She doesn't like the doctor.'

'OK, OK, Vicky, but remember, I'm here if you ever need anyone to talk to.'

After Lol had gone I cried into the pillow. I desperately wanted to tell Lol the truth as she seemed so kind, but how could I tell her what her boyfriend had done to me? How could a girl like Lol be fooled by my vicious, lying brother? How could she be so blind?

But maybe Lol wasn't the only one who was kidding herself?

The more Mum and Lol spoke about it, the more I thought about whether I could be pregnant. It definitely made sense. I'd had sex education at the last primary school I went to, and I knew how babies were formed. I wanted to make myself sick. The fear and dread built inside of me. It was a horrifying, stomach-wrenching thought – not only having a baby, but also having my brother's baby. It would make the whole nightmare ten times worse. So far I'd managed to push the humiliating ordeal aside and try, somehow, to get on with my life, but this would change everything. I wasn't sure how much more I could take. My mind felt like it was going to explode. Tears were on the verge of running down my face, every minute of every day. I was an emotional wreck. All I wanted was to play with Ben and be a normal kid again. I couldn't believe how much David had twisted my life out of shape. The only way I could get through it all was by going into complete denial.

A few hours later, after I'd had a little sleep, Mum came into the room and said we were going back to the doctors. 'Lol's mum said there's a lovely female doctor down the road who will slot us in tonight,' she said. I grabbed my shoes and coat and we headed down to see her. By now, I didn't know what to think. I was just totally shaken and I wanted to hide, and to never know the truth. I kept repeating to myself that there was no way I could be pregnant. It just couldn't happen.

As soon as we arrived at the doctor's surgery we were ushered into her room. She seemed lovely and Mum told her the situation as soon as we sat down.

'She's been having lots of pains,' she explained. 'We've been from one doctor to the next but she's still in pain. It's not right.' I just sat there, wishing I was anywhere else.

'OK, let's have a look shall we, Vicky? Do you want to hop onto the bed?' I did as I was asked and then she felt around my stomach. I looked at Mum and she smiled at me. Then there was silence. I watched the doctor's face. She was looking towards the ceiling one minute and then looking at me and smiling the next, while all the time she was poking and prodding my stomach. Then she pulled her hands away and ushered me back to my seat.

'Well, what do you think?' Mum interrogated her.

The doctor's voice was calm and professional. 'I'm afraid your daughter seems to be pregnant.'

Mum stared at me. I stared at the floor. 'Oh my God,' I thought. 'Oh my God! What am I going to do?'

'But she's twelve!' Mum said slowly, shaking her head in disbelief. 'How far gone is she?' she asked, taking my hand and squeezing it when the doctor answered 'About six months.'

It was like a nightmare. Six months since David raped me. Three months before my brother's child was due.

My mind quickly went into autopilot as I tried frantically to think of a believable excuse. There was no way I could stand here in this brightly lit room and tell them what my brother had done to me; what my mum's darling son had put me through. I didn't even digest the doctor's words properly. All I could think about was what I was going to say and how I was going to explain it. My mind was desperately searching out a story, something that would sound plausible. It was like no one else was in the room but me. Everything went quiet. Mum could've been shouting and going crazy, but I was oblivious; it was just me, my thoughts and the possible stories I was mentally grasping at to shield her from the truth.

Then I heard Mum's voice, cutting through my chaotic thoughts. She sounded like she was struggling to hold it together.

'Why didn't I guess earlier?' she kept saying. 'I should have guessed. I should have known.'

There was a mirror in the surgery. We all seemed to be staring at my tummy. I crossed my hands over it, defensively. But, physically, there were no real signs that I was six months gone. By that time I was quite a big girl anyway, and my size 16 clothes hung off me and disguised any lumps and bumps.

'It's often the way with very young mothers.' The doctor was matter-of-fact. 'It can be very hard to tell.'

Looking back, I see that we were all so shocked that everyone seemed to be skirting round the real issue. It was like the elephant in the room. Whether she had a bump or not, what the hell was a twelve-year-old doing being pregnant anyway?

'Have you been feeling anything in your stomach? Any butterfly sensations?' the doctor asked.

'Erm, yeah, I have,' I said. 'But I thought it was the bug.'

Mum clapped her hands over her mouth, as if she was trying to keep in a scream. For a moment I thought she was going to fall over, she was shaking so much. Instead she collapsed into a chair as the doctor booked me an appointment at the hospital the following morning, then she managed to struggle out the door when we had said our goodbyes.

After we walked out of the surgery, I braced myself for my mum to start shouting and bombarding me with questions. Instead she just walked ahead of me, her shoulders heaving, not even checking to see if I was following or not. I walked in a daze behind her. It felt like someone had turned off the sound of the outside world.

When we got home I ran straight up to my room. I didn't want to see anyone, especially David. I felt utterly ashamed, like I'd let everyone down. My door was ajar though and voices floated up from downstairs.

'What's up, love? You look like you've seen a ghost.' My dad's warm voice made me want to cry.

Mum's voice was much more brittle. 'I've got some news. You're going to be a grandfather.'

'Bloody hell, son, don't you think you and Lol are a little bit young for all that? Well, at least you're standing by her. A grandfather, eh? Thought that'd be a few years coming . . .'

He trailed off. Maybe he saw the look on Mum's face.

'What you on about?' David's voice was so loud that I jumped, looking round to check he hadn't somehow got into my room.

'It's not them,' Mum said.

'What the—?'

'It's Vicky. She's pregnant. Six months.'

Next thing I heard was pounding footsteps up the stairs. I cringed under the bedclothes. This was it: David was coming to get me. He knew I was carrying his baby, proof of his guilt, and he was coming to hurt me, to silence me for ever. The footsteps got closer and closer and the door was flung open. I readied myself to fight my depraved brother off.

But it wasn't David. It was Dad. He was standing in the doorway, looking much older and more fragile than I'd ever seen him look, even after his accident. Dad didn't say a word, he just sat on my bed and held me, hugging me tightly. It was the nicest feeling I'd had in ages. I wish he could've held me for ever. Stroking my back, he murmured into my hair: 'What have you been doing? You silly, silly little girl.' And that was it – the loving hug was lost. My whole body tensed and he drew away. His eyes were so full of disappointment that I couldn't look at him. It was so unfair! If only Dad knew I hadn't been a silly girl at all, that it wasn't my fault. But the words just couldn't leave my mouth. After so long, how could they? I'd buried them so deep. And yet how could I go on letting them think that I had been sleeping around, when I'd barely kissed a boy before? Part of me was angry. Didn't they even know their own daughter?

I never did find out how David reacted to the news. He never did come and find me and threaten me. He didn't have to. In a strange way, getting pregnant only confirmed his power over me. David could still destroy my life, months after the rape. I was getting bigger by the day but he didn't seem touched at all by what he had done to me. I found out later that, when Mum came in, he was sat on the sofa with Lol by his side. Mum said that, after Dad ran upstairs, he never said a word, never asked her a single question. Everyone was so shocked that she forgot to even look at my brother. I sometimes wonder what was going on inside his head. Was he proud? Did he think it was funny? Was even he dismayed by the consequences of his obscene attacks? Whatever the truth, outside – and maybe inside too – he was as cool as a cucumber. Even now, I hate the thought of him sitting there with Mum and Dad later that evening, calmly discussing my predicament when my parents had no idea of the horrible truth.

The next morning I went to the hospital, still feeling like I was walking around in a nightmare. I lay on the bed with my stomach covered in blue gunk, but I felt nothing when I saw movement on the monitor. I still hadn't accepted I had a baby inside of me, growing into an actual person. It seemed so alien and frightening to me. It just didn't seem real. That day I was told over and over again I was going to be a mum in three months, but I just sat blank-faced, staring into space, unable to take the news in. My own mum couldn't hide the tears welling up in her eyes. To her I was still a child – well, I *was* just a child – and it was too much for her to get her head around.

The doctor went on to talk about what would happen from then on and explain my options. 'What about a termination? How do you feel about that?' she asked. Even though I hadn't thought much about the foetus up until that moment, I knew I didn't want an abortion – I just couldn't kill the baby. The doctor went on to explain that, because I was so far gone, I'd still have to give birth if I had a termination. I would have to go through labour and see my dead baby at the end of it. That was all the confirmation I needed – scared as I was, there was no way I could do that. Mum agreed.

'That's an awful thing to have to go through,' she said, taking my hand very gently. She then looked at me carefully before continuing. 'Your Dad and me have already spoken and we'll be here for you. We can take care of the baby while you get on with your life. You know you can count on us.' Sitting there in the doctor's surgery we were both blinking back tears. I think that was the first time I felt any emotion towards the child – no matter how it was conceived, it was inside of me and it was now my baby.

I was so glad to have Mum. I clung to her in a way I hadn't done for years. She'd never, ever stood up for me like this before. Without her and Dad, I'd be utterly lost – I'd be on the streets, with my baby taken away from me. Or I'd be at David's mercy. Right then, in the hospital, I vowed that I would do whatever it took to keep their love and support, for my sake, but also for the sake of my baby. I hated David more than ever, but, if I wanted to stay with my family, I realised I'd have to abandon all hope of justice, revenge or even freedom from fear.

Neither Mum nor Dad had asked me yet who the father was. At the time I was too relieved to wonder why, but looking back I think that they were finding it so difficult getting their heads around me being pregnant that the question of how I got into that state would have been too much for them to handle. But if I thought I could carry on much longer without getting further enmeshed in a web of lies, I was wrong.

We'd barely got back from the hospital and sat down on the sofa when there was a knock at the door. It was the police. The hospital must've called social services, because I was so young. They told me I had to go down to the Banbury Police Station to give a statement. Mum looked so embarrassed as we trooped past all the neighbours and got into the police car. The officers were actually very kind, but we still looked like criminals. When we got there the police told me I had to tell them everything. Sitting in the interview room, it felt like I was the one being punished. Mum sat next to me as I told one story after the other, thinking of things really quickly. I was terrified and knew I couldn't be making much sense. All I knew was that I had to keep my secret, had to keep silent the words that would destroy my family. The police wanted to know who the father was and where he lived. How could I tell them it was my brother, and that he'd be waiting for us at home?

On the spur of the moment, I thought of Robin, my little boyfriend from the caravan park. I told them he was the father. That one lie wasn't enough for the police though. I had to tell them how I met him, as well as what kind of a relationship we had. Mum and Dad were still in touch with his parents so I had to sit back while Mum gave them their address and number. As soon as I'd said Robin's name I wished I'd come up with some other story. I felt so guilty for blaming my poor, innocent friend, but I was panic-stricken. On the spur of the moment his name was the first that came to hand. In fact, it was such a convincing story and I was made to repeat it so many times, that even I started to believe it.

People say that evil begets evil, and to this day I find it hard to forgive myself for dragging Robin into my sad situation. Even then I knew he didn't deserve to get caught up in it all, and now I'm older I regret it even more. It was a terrible thing to do and must have caused him and his family a great deal of distress. But I was so young and naïve and scared, and, once the words were out of my mouth I couldn't go back on them. There's no excuse for blaming an innocent person, but I hoped that, if Robin ever knew the truth, he'd understand what an impossible situation I was in.

One of the police officers asked Mum if she would step outside of the interview room for a minute. 'I won't be long, sweetheart,' she said. I sat silently with another officer, and waited. Were they talking about me? Had they realised I was lying? A flush of shame swept across my cheeks. After only a few minutes, Mum came back into the interview room with the officer. She took my hand. 'I'm going to ask you something now, Vicky,' she said, rather flustered. 'Are you sure you're not protecting anyone in the family?'

I looked at her, confused. Did she know something? Was this my chance? I cleared my throat to speak, and Mum visibly crumpled. She was like a balloon that I had popped with a pin. I couldn't do it. I couldn't do it to her.

'No, of course not,' I said, my blush deepening.

'They think it's Dad,' Mum whispered.

I suddenly felt weak and dizzy.

'What? No way. Dad hasn't done anything. He would never do anything like that,' I sobbed. I couldn't believe they were thinking Dad could be capable of something so horrible. How dare they accuse him of that!

'It's all right. It's OK, young lady. We do just have to check these things.' The policeman's voice was soothing, and he got out a pen to get started on the paperwork.

Now I'm older and I think back, it should've been obvious that something was wrong and that someone in my family was responsible for getting me pregnant. I was in such a state, inventing stories so wildly. But no one picked up on it. I suppose it was easier for the police to write me off as just another teen pregnancy from the wrong side of the tracks.

Part of me was relieved no one noticed, glad they didn't dig any deeper. But another part of me wanted the authorities to keep asking me questions and find out the truth so I didn't have to keep the awful secret to myself any longer. I didn't really know what I wanted, I just knew I wanted someone else to take all the confusion and hatred away, to make all the decisions for me, and then give me back my old life. I didn't want to be mature and deal with so much seriousness. I wanted to be an innocent child again.

We eventually left the station and when we got home Dad was waiting for me with another big hug. David and Lol were still there. My stomach kept flipping like a pancake at the thought of what was going on in David's head. Would he get angry and persuade me to get rid of the baby? Or, even worse, would he relish the thought of becoming a dad and uncle at the same time? There was no way I could let him play his twisted game of happy families with me. I felt so out of control, as though my life wasn't my own any more. And, in an important way, it wasn't – there was the baby to think of too. Clinging to this thought, I managed to find a mask to cover my anguish. 'I just have to get on with it,' I told myself. But still, I would've done anything to turn the clocks back and be that little girl who played with Ben every minute of the day. Being a mother is a huge, daunting role, and as a traumatised twelve-year-old, there was no way I was ready to play it.

I needn't have wasted energy worrying about how my brother would react, however. David didn't say anything to me. There was never even a flicker of acknowledgement that the baby was his. It was like I'd imagined those nightmarish nights, like I'd conjured up this baby all by myself. I continued to avoid any possible eye contact. The last thing I wanted was for him to say anything to me. We hadn't really spoken at all since the attacks, other than the bare minimum. I have no idea what David did in the privacy of his own room, or what he felt in the depths of his conscience. Maybe he cried, maybe he laughed. I'll never know how he felt about the news that he'd fathered a child with his baby sister.

I later found out that the police contacted Robin's parents and told them what I had said. Obviously they were shocked; even more so when Robin denied everything. But I just stuck to my story, which made Robin seem like a liar. I feel so guilty about that now. If I saw him again I'd tell him how sincerely sorry I am; it was a dreadful thing to do. But I was a little girl and I was like a frightened, trapped bird. I just wanted to stop my family from falling apart. Thankfully, the police didn't take it any further, because Robin was so young too. I made Dad promise not to confront him as well, so we never heard from Robin or his family ever again. I was Mum and Dad's main priority now and the situation was bad enough, as far as they were concerned, without thinking too deeply about how I'd gotten pregnant.

Over the next few weeks I was sure David was going to find an opportunity to corner me and have it out with me, so I made sure I was surrounded by people all of the time. I was convinced he'd threaten me, blame me for falling pregnant. Whenever he was close, I'd walk away or start talking to someone else. I never spoke to him. I often wondered if Mum and Dad noticed, but then I'd hear Mum say to David: 'Leave Vicky alone, love. Her hormones are all over the place. It's nothing personal.' It drove me mad. Part of me wanted them to know the real reason why I hated my brother, and make them see how much disgust I had for him. But now, more than ever, it seemed impossible to break my silence. I was so vulnerable, and my unborn baby was even more vulnerable still. It was a no win situation, and I felt completely trapped. The lie had gone so far now that there was no way out, no chance of going back. It felt like I'd lied so much that no one would ever trust me again.

David's girlfriend carried on being lovely. If she was shocked that I'd got pregnant so young, she didn't let on, and she really tried to be there for me. We'd chat and she'd be nice to me, but then, as soon as David would join her, I'd walk away. It was a crying shame that she was with my violent, devious brother. In a way I felt guilty, letting such a nice girl be blinded by David's charm when I knew exactly how dangerous he was. But, in the end, even I underestimated how much danger she was in.

For the next three months the constant sickness never subsided, and seemed to be particularly bad when I was in David's presence. There were even times when I had got so close to David that I had to rush off to the toilet to put my fingers down my throat and make myself sick, because the feeling in my stomach was so heavy that throwing up was the only thing that would help. It felt like a constant battle just to get through each day.

As my belly swelled, memories of the rape got buried deeper and deeper inside of me. The more people I told about the boy from the caravan park, the more real it seemed. It became such a convincing lie that I ended up wanting to believe it myself. It was definitely a better story than the real one about my own brother creeping into my room at night. Standing next to David still sent shivers down my spine, but it was a case of mind over matter. As I concentrated on keeping calm for the baby's sake, I tried to force my mind to forget what he'd done to me.

By then, school was non-existent. I hadn't really been going much anyway, but now we knew I was pregnant the authorities agreed I should stay at home. I spent most of my time with Ben during the last three months of my pregnancy. He was permanently by my side, as soon as I went to sleep at night and first thing in the morning; he was my constant protector. Also, because I was pregnant, my parents started spending much more time with me, worrying and fussing. It made me feel safe. For the first time in my life I always had someone near me making sure I was OK.

Not everyone was as kind and caring as my parents were, though. Every time I left the house, to buy a pint of milk or get a newspaper for Dad, I felt like I was under attack. Kids my own age would shout names at me, while groups of older lads would jeer and wolf-whistle at me as I tried to cover up my growing bump. Even for a village where there were quite a few teenage mums, the sight of a heavily pregnant twelve-year-old was a freak show for passers-by. Even some of my parents' friends would tut at me. I overheard one woman say: 'Such a shame about Vicky. She always seemed like such a nice little thing.'

'Still, it's always the quiet ones, isn't it?' the shopkeeper remarked, handing her some change. 'If she was my girl she'd get such a hiding she'd think twice about messing around with boys again for a few years.'

'It's the parents I feel sorry for. It must be terrible for them. A young girl like that getting herself in the family way . . .'

They'd trail off, embarrassed, when they noticed me at the other end of the aisle. I tried to look like I didn't care, but inside I was burning with the unfairness of it all. David had raped me, and now it was me who was being punished, me who was dragging the family name through the mud.

The terrible thing was that part of me agreed with her. Part of me felt so dirty because of what David had done to me that I felt like I deserved all their harsh words. In fact, sometimes it was the pitying looks that were harder to take.

When I look back at those few months, it scares me how quickly I had to grow up and change. I celebrated my thirteenth birthday just a couple of months before I gave birth, but it was like no other birthday we'd ever had in the house. I'd never been one for parties and games because I never had a lot of friends around, but, still, that day had a cloud over it that confirmed that life was never going to be the same. It seemed no time at all since I'd been playing with my Tiny Tears baby doll, and now I was supposed to be planning for my own baby. Sometimes I'd forget it was even happening, and then I'd suddenly get catapulted into reality by the baby kicking. It was a very surreal time for me. I still wanted to be a child, but life kept reminding me that I couldn't be.

The last month of my pregnancy was spent thinking of names and trying to prepare for motherhood. I had to visit the hospital a few times, to have ante-natal classes and learn what was ahead, but I was so mentally removed that I was in complete denial that I had a baby inside me. I was at least ten years younger than most of the women in the classes, and by the way they stopped talking when I walked into the room, I knew they were all gossiping about me. I also had to get some maternity wear from Mothercare, as my huge stomach kept expanding. The shop assistant could barely bring herself to look at me let alone help me. She made it very clear that the likes of me were not welcome in her store.

The only part I did enjoy about the pregnancy was the chance to think of names. Like any young girl, I liked choosing names for new possessions, and for me that's how I imagined the baby. The thought that it would be its own little personality hadn't even properly occurred to me. I had decided the name if it was a boy – James Leonard Alan, after Dad. Girl's names were proving more tricky to decide, however, so one night I made a list of my favourites and sent it round the pub. I remember that one of the regular punters walked out when he saw me there, so heavily pregnant. When I saw his shocked face, I wanted to cry. Mum quickly shushed me, glaring a warning at the rest of the room, daring them to upset me one little bit. The whispers quieted down after that and, eventually, the list came back to me. It seemed everyone liked the name Kirsty, so that was it – my decision had been made. It was a beautiful name. But I had no idea how beautiful my baby was going to be and whether I would be able to accept it or not. Life seemed so out of control, and I was desperately worried about whether a baby conceived in hate could bring anything but more pain and heartbreak.

8

My Beautiful Baby

On 26 July 1987 we had just moved to the Carpenters Arms in Trowbridge. It was a lovely town, with plenty of shops nearby and a police station just opposite the pub. But the pub had lots of stairs – not ideal for a heavily pregnant girl like me. One day I ended up slipping, catching my foot in the wooden banister and doing the splits down eight steps. I ended up falling, bang, into the door that led into the main pub. 'Oh my God,' Mum yelled, as she ran over.

'What happened?'

Dad helped me onto my feet as I giggled with shock. I hadn't hurt myself and now I couldn't stop laughing.

'I'm all right. I'll survive,' I managed to say between giggles.

But Mum wasn't smiling. 'Now, tell us if you get any pains or cramps. God knows how the fall affected the baby,' she warned, frowning.

'Do you reckon we should get her checked out?' Dad asked, looking terrified. Everyone worried so much about the baby that I felt a little cast aside. From then on I started to face facts that this was the way my life was now: the baby came first. It was hard to get used to that when I was still really only a child myself and wanted attention and love too.

With just weeks to go until my due date, Mum had a lot of friends staying to be sure we were all prepared for any eventuality. She'd already fallen out with one friend over me, so everyone was careful to mind their ps and qs while she was in the room. But I do remember one woman from the village who really upset me.

Late one night she came upstairs smelling of wine and just stood in the doorway looking at me.

'Don't let this ruin your life, Vicky. You're just a little girl. Just a little girl . . . What were you thinking of? Next time, learn to say no.'

Her voice was gentle, but her words still burnt into my brain. And the more people assumed that it was all my fault, the more I started to believe it too.

Another night, after the pub had shut, we were all in Mum's bedroom chatting. I'd been sleeping with Mum for weeks and Dad was in my bed – Mum wanted me to be close to her, in case I had any problems. I was exhausted. I had my long flowing nightie on, ready for bed, and for a minute I felt so happy and playful that I pulled on my favourite Dr Martens boots for a joke and told everyone I was going to bed. They all fell down laughing. For a moment we looked like a normal family. Then I looked down at my straining belly in the childish nightie, and I remembered how horribly twisted our family had become.

That night we went to bed and I had a good night's sleep. In the morning Mum went downstairs and prepared breakfast, coming up with a tray full of toast and cups of tea. We were all sitting on the bed eating when suddenly I felt some cramps in my stomach. Mum quickly took control and was dead calm as she called an ambulance. I was petrified, terrified of how much the labour was going to hurt. Thankfully, David was at his girlfriend's house, so I didn't need to worry about him leering over me.

By 8.30am I was in an ambulance on the way to Bath Royal Hospital – Trowbridge's local hospital didn't feel fully equipped to deal with a thirteen-year-old mother. It took us about two hours to get there, going round bendy country roads. It was a hellish journey. Mum stayed by my side, helping me breathe and keep calm. It felt like it was never going to end. The pain would come and go with the contractions. And it was like someone knocking the wind out of me – I'd never felt anything like it. I cried my eyes out and clung to my mum's hand.

Dad stayed at the pub with the locals and called all the family to come down and wait together. I later found out that David joined them too, waiting for news like a proud uncle. I found that so hard to accept. Images of him sipping a celebratory pint with my dad made my skin crawl. It was such a difficult position to be in – I was desperate to tell everyone what David was like and how much of a fraud he was, but where would that leave me? The lies had become the truth in some ways, and it was becoming harder and harder to retract my story. But having my rapist wait with the rest of the family for the news of his child's birth was just too cruel to take in.

At Bath Hospital I was taken into the labour ward and we just waited. The midwives were lovely and took extra care of me, because I was so young. They could fully understand how scared I was, being little more than a kid myself. Hours passed and nothing happened. Eventually, they realised my water wasn't breaking on its own so they cut a hole and then we waited again. But by 2pm there was still no sign of more labour pains. Mum suggested my water had re-sealed, and it had. They cut a hole again and that was it, the labour began. I was so scared. I had no idea what to expect and how bad the pain was going to get. All

I could do was concentrate on what the midwives were telling me. As soon as they said breathe, I breathed, and as soon as they said push, I pushed. I hung on their every word, a scared little girl out of her depth.

After two hours of pushing as hard as I could with my legs up in stirrups, I gave birth to a bawling little girl. She just kind of plopped out. It was such a weird feeling. Everyone fussed around me and was happy for me. In that brief moment they seemed to forget how young I was. They expected me to act like a proud mother, but I was still in shock and didn't even want to hold my baby.

'Oh, Vicky, you have a beautiful, healthy daughter. Get your arms ready and hold her head,' they said.

I flinched and the midwife backed off. 'No, it's OK. Give her to Mum,' I said. Mum took the baby and smiled at her and then shoved her little sleepy face in front of me.

'Look, Vicky, she's perfect. She looks like a Kirsty – just beautiful.' And as I tried looking at her some more, I agreed – she was beautiful – and I finally smiled. She was perfect. David had left no mark on her. Mainly, though, I was just relieved it was all over. It just didn't feel real. I couldn't believe I was the baby's mother.

Mum seemed besotted with Kirsty, but I was still trying to take in what I'd just experienced. While Mum held on to Kirsty and talked to her, I had 195 stitches to sew my ravaged reproductive parts back up. The doctor said it was like putting a jigsaw back together. I was torn to pieces, because my little thirteen-year-old body couldn't cope with the labour. The doctor tried to make a joke out of everything and keep the atmosphere jolly, but we all knew how bad those stitches sounded. Having a baby at thirteen just shouldn't happen.

Three hours after the birth, I held my baby for the first time, but only for ten minutes. All I could think was how wrinkly and old she looked. She didn't look like anyone in particular, just like an alien. I was so relieved that she didn't remind me of David – she was her own little person. At that moment I knew I loved everything about her. She was conceived in the most tragic way but she made everything beautiful. I made a promise to myself, as I looked at her adorable nose and held her tiny fingers, that she would never know the truth. I never wanted her to know that her mummy was attacked so brutally and put through so much anguish, and that she was the result of incestuous rape. It'd be hard for any person to accept that, and Kirsty was so adorable that I didn't want her to have any part of my pain.

I spent the first twenty-four hours after giving birth trying to sleep, while Mum looked after Kirsty. Thankfully, she was allowed to stay with me on the ward. I don't know what I would've done without her. Early that evening I woke up and I held Kirsty a bit more. For a few minutes it felt like nothing terrible had happened and I was just a young girl who had got pregnant, with her mum by her side. But then flashes of history would bolt through my mind and every time I shut my eyes I thought I smelt David's sickly sweet deodorant.

The following day Mum and I had to be moved back to Trowbridge Hospital. Staff waved us off and gave me lots of hugs. I was really thankful for how they'd been with me – truly wonderful. Mum said Dad was picking us up but as we waited for our lift David and Lol showed up instead. It was a huge shock because I hadn't prepared myself for seeing him so soon, and I was so weak that I was worried that I'd fall down on the hospital steps. Mum was all excited though, showing off Kirsty, and Lol was acting like a proud auntie. My heart was in my mouth. I didn't know what to do or how to behave, I was so shocked.

'Look, David, look at your little niece,' Mum said, holding her up. I wanted to scream: 'Stay away from her!' But how could I? How could I try to explain, after all the lies I'd told? Thankfully, David just looked at her and walked away without saying a word. I grabbed Kirsty and wrapped her in my arms, trying to stop myself from shaking.

Since the rapes I always made sure that my brother and I never made eye contact, and this time was no different. I couldn't imagine what would happen if we caught one another's eye. The thought of us being proud parents disgusted me and made me feel sick. Even though I had just given birth to his daughter, I hated him even more than ever. I just acted like Kirsty was mine, and only mine. The more I told myself that, the more I believed it and the easier it was to share a car with David back to Trowbridge. I had spent the last month of my pregnancy worrying about the day when David would meet our child, and it was even worse than I had ever imagined.

After an hour of driving, Mum decided to take a detour. 'Let's pop home,' she suggested. As soon as we walked through the pub doors, everyone applauded and cheered. There was none of the tutting and whispering that was to come later. As it was an unannounced arrival of course people were a bit shocked, but the regulars were lovely. Dad came running towards us and he couldn't take his eyes off Kirsty – it was adorable to watch. Everyone was coming up to me and congratulating me. It actually felt nice, until I saw, in the corner of my eye, that David was still lurking in the background.

Eventually, we had to leave and head back to the hospital before my bed was taken by another patient. I was still in a lot of pain and couldn't walk properly so hospital was the safest place for me. As soon as we arrived I got comfortable and Mum prepared Kirsty for her cot, but next minute one of the sisters came over.

'C'mon, hurry up, there's no time to change her into her babygro I'm afraid, love. Just put her down; visiting hours are over,' she said. Mum and I looked at one another. I must've looked like I was going to cry.

'Please don't leave me, Mum,' I said, shakily. The sister just looked at us.

'I'm sorry,' Mum continued. 'But I'm not leaving my thirteen-year-old daughter on her own. I'm staying here, right beside her.' The sister turned on her heels and walked back to reception mumbling to herself. Mum followed. I waited in bed for news, desperately hoping they weren't going to send Mum home. I couldn't do this alone. Then just as I was really starting to panic, Mum came back with another sister and patted my arm.

'It's fine darling, this lovely nurse is going to sort out a bed for me.'

I breathed a huge sigh of relief, and beamed a grateful smile at my mum before falling asleep. I was exhausted.

My relationship with Mum had been such a rollercoaster ride for so long, but throughout the pregnancy and birth, I got the chance to see a completely different side to her. I was used to her being a bit cold and distant with me, but now I was getting a taste of the love and loyalty that she usually lavished on David. If Mum hadn't been there, I would've been lost – she had been a tower of strength for me. But still, I wondered how long it was going to last. Mum's actions had never been consistent: one minute she was full of hugs and love; next she was as cold as ice. And even though she had been great through the past few months, I worried about how genuine she was – was it a chance for Mum to enjoy being in control again? They were thoughts I would've preferred not to be thinking, but I couldn't help it; it was what Mum had led me to expect. I had always been brought up surrounded by the notion that family came first, no matter what, and even though Mum was following the rule, her hugs and kind words didn't always feel like they were from the heart. The affectionate cuddles and reassuring looks from her were never as convincing as they were coming from Dad. It was sad, but it was what I was used to. Mum was there for me – for now. Soon her attentions would be caught up in something else, and I dreaded the day when I would lose her to David again.

When Dad arrived for another visit the day after we arrived at Trowbridge hospital, I was overjoyed, but he looked like death warmed up-something perhaps explained by the fact that it was his birthday the day before!

'What's wrong with you?' Mum asked him.

'Might have had a drink or two last night.'

'Just one or two?' I asked cheekily.

'Actually, I feel like I've got the worst hangover in history,' Dad admitted, sitting down unsteadily. 'But it's not every day you turn forty and become a granddad.'

It felt weird that Dad had been celebrating the birth of his granddaughter, thinking it was fabulous news. But, on the other hand, I wanted to believe what he believed – that everything was normal and I'd just given birth to a gorgeous, healthy little girl. I didn't want to remember any of the badness now Kirsty was here. Even though Dad had found it hard to accept that his baby girl was pregnant to begin with, he was now over the moon. Kirsty was a beautiful addition to the family, and all I had to do was keep David away from her – somehow.

Mum and I stayed in hospital for a week, talking and cooing over little Kirsty. It gave me a chance to learn what to do without the pressure of being at home. It was also a relief not having to worry about when David was going to pop his head round the corner as I knew he wouldn't dare show his face at the hospital. Plus, it gave me the chance for my ravaged body to recover a little. I was still in agony and every day I forced myself to swallow down a cocktail of painkillers. If I ever wanted to sit up, I had to sit on a doughnut-shaped cushion, and even that was uncomfortable. But it was better than the unbearable pain of sitting full force on my bottom. The sharp pain reminded me uncomfortably of what David had done to me, but I tried as hard as I could to banish those poisonous thoughts from my mind.

Dad came to pick us up a full week after Kirsty was born. As I sat in the back seat, cradling my precious baby, I made a promise to her: she would never be hurt in the way that I had. Whatever it took, I would keep her away from David. She was mine, and I would protect her with my life. Right then I felt as fierce as a lioness with her cub. If only I could have held on to that bravery. But, as we pulled into our street, the sickening dread of seeing David began to eat away at my courage. I hadn't been able to protect myself from him, so how the hell could I protect this vulnerable, innocent little person I held so tightly in my arms?

When we got to the pub, it was full of family and friends waiting to welcome us home. For a few moments my fears evaporated. It was lovely to be surrounded by good friends and wonderful family, and people were so generous, bringing loads of presents for the baby. Kirsty was passed around everyone to be adored, and I managed to stay and absorb the atmosphere, sitting on my doughnut cushion. More than ever I wanted to believe everything was OK, that there was nothing to be frightened of. Then David walked in. My first instinct was to turn and run, dragging my baby and my battered body out of the room. Since having Kirsty my physical fear of him had worsened. I could actually feel the terror pumping through my veins now, as if the rapes had only just happened. But Kirsty was on the other side of the pub, and this was supposed to be our homecoming celebrations. I forced myself to stay still and silent as my brother made his way over to the bar, wearing a sleazy grin on his face. My stomach kept flipping and I was worried I'd be sick. He never tried to talk to me, but his penetrating stares were still enough to terrify me.

After that first tense afternoon at home David went back to Bloxham to stay with Lol. It was a huge relief when Mum told me. It meant I could fuss over Kirsty and not wonder if he was spying on us from a distance. I was also able to move around a lot more, have baths, or go for little walks to help my recovery. Mum was great. She took over looking after Kirsty while my body was still healing, but it didn't affect the bonding between Kirsty and me. Despite the terrible way she came into the world, and the traumatic birth, I loved Kirsty more than anything in the world and we spent a lot of quality time together, having cuddles. All I had to do was keep her safe from David, and if I managed that, I was sure we could be happy.

As soon as we were home, Dad went out to buy everything – cot, pram, bottles, steriliser, toys. He was great. Whatever I needed, he went to get. I suppose it seemed crazy that we hadn't got prepared before the birth, but it had all happened so quickly. I had been deeply in denial, and shopping was the last thing on anybody's mind.

I was back on my feet when Kirsty was about four weeks old, and then I started to do a lot more for her. I fed her, got her ready for bed and dressed her. The only thing I didn't have the confidence to do was bath her. I hated holding her slippery little body in my arms. I was terrified that I was going to drop her, or she was going to slip through my fingers and drown. So Mum had to take over in that department, but otherwise she left me to it and I surprised myself by doing a great job. I'd gotten so used to being called a 'thicko' that it was wonderful to find something that I was good at.

Although I enjoyed being a new mother, I was soon reminded that there were many people who were far from happy for me. While I'd been pregnant I hadn't really thought about the effect that having a baby would have on my life. At the end of the day, I only had about three months to get used to the idea, after all, and I was still traumatised from my experiences with David, so what other people thought wasn't really on my list of worries. Coming back from the hospital it was only my brother's reaction I worried about. I honestly thought my only problem would be keeping my daughter away from him. But then, as soon as I started to venture out in the world with Kirsty, reality set in.

I really wasn't prepared for the fact that so many people would look down on me for being a thirteen-year-old girl with a baby. I was little more than a kid myself, and it affected me more than perhaps it should have. I was hurt and embarrassed by other people's vicious reactions, and in the end I didn't have the confidence to go out with Kirsty in the daytime. Grown adults would call me a slag, and say I was dirty or easy. I couldn't believe people could be so cruel. Hadn't I got enough to deal with already? It got so bad that I was scared to step outside the front door; so, when Kirsty was still very young, I hid away and let Mum take over when it came to dealing with the world outside our home.

Sometimes Mum, Dad and I took Kirsty out in the pram when we walked the dogs after the pub closed. The thought of facing anyone in the daytime terrified me so it was lucky it was summer at that time and still warm at night. We went to the park, or the canal, and it was lovely. Still, part of me raged that I couldn't bring Kirsty out to enjoy the sunshine. Why should me and my baby suffer when David was free to walk about whenever he wanted?

As Kirsty was a summer baby we often sat in the back garden. Ben and Taura were also very protective of Kirsty. One afternoon, I was in the kitchen and I could hear Kirsty whinging. By the time I got outside, Taura had her paws up on the pram. I screamed and ran over, terrified that the dog would hurt her, but Taura was just tapping Kirsty's legs to try and comfort her. It was unbelievable. Once I'd recovered from the shock, I thought it was really cute and called Mum over to show her.

Having Mum and Dad with me during those first few weeks was a massive support. They kept me grounded and helped me feel I was still normal. In some ways, Mum acted like Kirsty's second mother. As a mum of four, it was natural for her to take over at first, but, as soon as I wanted to do my share, she stepped aside. It was a brilliant partnership, and in those first few weeks it just worked. It was sometimes hard to believe that this was the same

Mum I'd been terrified of confiding in. If only she had let me see this side of her when I was the one who needed looking after.

Many days Kirsty slept in her bouncy chair under a speaker in the pub – she loved music and always fell asleep as soon as a tune came on. Kirsty was a brilliant distraction for me. I'd had so many months of misery, nightmares, fear and uncertainty. Now I was only thinking of her, and anything else was a distant worry. There had been times when I didn't know if I could survive feeling so many awful feelings and experiencing so many horrific thoughts, but I went on because I had a baby inside of me. I think I would've killed myself if it hadn't been for Kirsty. She brought happiness into my life at a very dark time, a time when I desperately needed it.

9

Growing Up

When Kirsty was just six weeks old, Mum and Dad were told that the brewery they worked for had gone bankrupt and that there was no more work for them. It was a terrible shock: we would be homeless just when we needed a roof over our heads the most. After a lot of sleepless nights, my parents found us a room in a temporary council-run B&B in Southend-on-Sea. 'See, I told you we'd be ok,' Dad reassured me one day. 'You know I'd never let you down,' he joked with a cheeky wink. And, yes, I did know that in my heart of hearts. Dad always came up trumps; he was a father to be proud of.

'But what about work, Dad?' I asked. Without a pub to run they didn't have any income, which was a real worry now we had Kirsty to take care of too.

'Got it sorted. A few mates are going to give me shifts and holiday cover – nothing for you to worry about. You just concentrate on getting back on your feet,' he added.

The first six weeks was a matter of slow, painful recovery. My body had been through so much I wasn't even capable of holding Kirsty for any more than a short time, because of the pressure on my wounds. I used to sit back and watch Mum fuss over Kirsty and it fascinated me. So many people melt at the sight of a cute baby, but I still couldn't connect with that, not even over my own little girl. I was just a child myself, I suppose, and I just hadn't grown up enough yet to connect love and the ability to mother. I was in denial. I couldn't accept I was a mum yet and that I had to provide for this child. Mum continued to encourage my involvement, though, and was always asking me my opinion or getting me to help as much as I could. But, as the weeks passed, my early confidence left me and I became increasingly scared of doing something wrong and hurting Kirsty.

'Do you want to give me a hand changing her today?' Mum'd ask.

'No, it's OK, Mum, you go ahead,' I'd reply.

'You will in time, darling,' Mum would sigh, patting me on the shoulder. I wanted to believe that she was right, but as my confidence was at such a low ebb, it felt safer to let her care for my vulnerable baby.

Through a friend, Dad thankfully carried on getting some work at other pubs, while Mum, Kirsty and I stayed at the B&B. Dad never let us down. Secretly, I was happy about the move, because it meant we were even further away from David, who we'd left behind in Bloxham. To my huge relief, we saw him less and less. But whenever he did visit, the familiar panic would surge through me and it would take me days to get over it.

Over the next seven months Dad moved around every two or three weeks and occasionally I would go and stay with him, or all three of us joined him for a little holiday.

But, as the weeks passed, something inside of me started to change. As soon as Kirsty was in bed at night, I'd hang out in the pub and I began to mix with boys a few years older. I felt very different to how I used to before David attacked me. I didn't feel like the child who sat in the corner of the room any more, hiding from everyone. I mixed with people a few years older than me and made out like I was sixteen. I began to flirt with them and I became a bit of a tease, something I had never done before. I think I was testing the boundaries. When my older brother raped me, he flung my life into fast-forward and I'd been forced to grow up terrifyingly fast.

In many ways, having Kirsty was more difficult for me than anyone really realised. I had imagined starting a family when I was happy and content as an adult, not at such a young age, under such appalling circumstances. My relationship with my own mother had been distant, and I felt like I didn't even know what motherly instincts were. But still, I loved Kirsty and wanted to do my best. As the situation sunk in I became exhausted with the struggle to be maternal, and perhaps I stopped trying so hard. After all that had happened to me, I just wanted to be young and silly.

Even though I tried my best to block it out, Kirsty reminded me of David. Although she didn't look like him, it was difficult to look at Kirsty without remembering what David had done to me and, although I constantly reminded myself that it wasn't her fault, sometimes I struggled to forget who her real father was. I was only thirteen years old so, although I adored Kirsty, I was not ready to be a mother. After a nightmarish year, I felt like I deserved some fun.

I started to develop bad habits. Once, when we were staying over at a pub that Dad was looking after, I stayed up after my parents had gone to bed to watch a film with one of Dad's friends, Mike. He was smoking a joint. The smell was sweet and exotic, and he looked so relaxed.

'Mike, could I have a try of that?' I said, nervous that he'd be annoyed.

'If you want, love.' He looked me over. 'But I think you're a bit young for that sort of thing. I'm not sure your dad would like it.'

'Go on, give me some!' I smiled. My heart was racing. Even though I'd had to grow up really fast, I'd never done anything illegal before.

'Oh, all right, then. Guess it won't do any harm.' He passed it over and I had a couple of puffs, coughing on the unfamiliar smoke. In a few minutes I was so stoned I couldn't stand. I crawled to bed, giggling.

'Shhh!' Mike looked worried. 'Your parents will kill me if they wake up and find you in this state.' But I didn't care. That night I had the first solid night's sleep in nearly a year. For once I went to sleep without bad memories from the past floating around my head and keeping me awake. I realised that life could be a little more relaxed with joints around and that was the start of a very long addiction.

My parents had no idea that I'd ever smoked a cigarette, never mind anything stronger. Mum eventually found out that I'd started smoking when she came across a packet of cigarettes in a small bathroom cupboard.

'Vicky, if you don't want me to find something, don't hide it somewhere I go,' she said, slamming them down on the kitchen table. I was waiting for a lecture, but it never came. I think she was wary of giving me a hard time because she felt bad that I'd been through the awful experience of giving birth so young, and for that reason she also saw me as, essentially, an adult. Unfortunately, I wasn't behaving like an adult. Increasingly, the shy, scared little girl was turning into a confused and angry rebel.

As the months passed, I felt like a completely different person. I had dealt with so much on my own for so long and I'd had enough. I wanted life to be more adventurous. It felt like the old Vicky had gone and a new braver, brasher person had taken her place. I developed a tough exterior, but all the torment and secrecy of the past few years were just pushed deeper and deeper inside me.

I started to go down to the seafront in Southend-on-Sea to hang out. Mum and Dad had no idea where I went. Most of the time I told them I was taking Ben for a walk, but instead I was hanging out with local boys. I'd smoke and flirt in front of the arcades and stay out until late. Despite my more confident exterior, I had such low self-esteem that I craved male attention.

I think Mum and Dad were glad that I was mixing with the locals and having some fun while they looked after Kirsty, but I really started to go down a slippery slope to nowhere. Thankfully, I wasn't that interested in alcohol – being so young, I didn't like the taste – but I smoked cannabis instead. I liked the way it completely numbed my brain and I had no idea what I was doing.

Kirsty was still a tiny baby when I started my first adult relationship. I say adult, but I was barely a teenager. Looking back, I can't believe I rushed into it so quickly, but I was like a needy child, craving love and attention. His name was Rob and he was twenty, while I was still only thirteen. He lived in the B&B and I got very friendly with him and his brother. I let them assume I was older too, and we were very flirty with one another. I really liked Rob and we spent a lot of time together, smoking in our flowery wallpapered B&B rooms. It was amazing to be close to someone again, but soon we became more than friends. On night we kissed and held one another, and from then on we were a couple. I loved his tenderness and he made me feel so protected. But the closer we became the more I became convinced that Rob would eventually want to sleep with me. It was going to be the first time I'd had sex since David raped me. Part of me hated the thought of anyone touching me like that, but there was also a reckless part of me that thought that nothing mattered now that David had stolen my innocence. Deep down, I think I blamed myself for what David had done to me and I had so little self-respect that I didn't think I was worth more. So, when I should have been playing spin the bottle with boys my own age, I was getting ready to start a sexual relationship with a grown man.

Even at thirteen I thought that sex was what men really wanted; and in my head I believed they'd take it even if you didn't want to give it to them. So, in my little immature mind, I concluded that, to get more attention and love from Rob I'd have to give him sex. I look back and feel so sad that I was so desperate for someone to love me, but I was so young and damaged I didn't know any better.

One afternoon we were alone in Rob's room and one thing led to another. I was so scared it'd hurt again that I just wanted it out of the way. 'Please hurry up,' I kept saying to myself. 'Let it be over soon.' I just lay there as he did what he wanted. Initially I worried that I'd feel like I did with David, but thankfully it was very different. It was more tender and, because Rob kissed me a lot, if felt nicer. More importantly, I felt in control this time because I'd made the decision to put myself in that position, rather than being the weak, scared little girl that I was with David.

Afterwards, Rob just held me and that was what I'd been waiting for – in my mind, it showed that to get the love and affection I craved I had to provide sex. It was the only way I could understand it. I still couldn't think of sex as a nice act, because I could only understand it as a way of having power over someone. I didn't orgasm or have any feelings of enjoyment, so it was something that had to be done for me to get to the parts that I enjoyed: the loving and hugging. Now I look back and feel so sad that David had twisted my ideas about sex so much that I didn't feel like I could say no and still be loved.

Mum, Kirsty and I continued following Dad around to numerous pubs. It was all I knew by now; we'd done it for most of my life so I'd never really known what it was like to settle and put down roots. But now I didn't just have myself to think about. I didn't want Kirsty to have a life like that. I couldn't stand the thought of her being lonely and I hated seeing her confusion as we moved from one place to another. The constant upheaval was exhausting and I rarely had the energy to leave the pub and meet up with my friends. Instead I'd hang out in the bar, swapping smart retorts and innuendo with the customers, who responded to me as an attractive, blossoming woman, not the attention-seeking little girl I was inside.

Once we joined Dad at a pub in Chitterne, near Stonehenge, in Warminster. It was a lovely little village with farms and lots of animals. We bought two little lambs and they kept walking around the pub – they were so adorable.

By now I was confident enough to speak to just about any adult, and became very friendly and flirty with the regulars. Then one night a lady came crashing through the doors shouting abuse at me.

'You're having an affair with my husband!' she screamed. 'I've seen the letters.'

I was stunned; I didn't know what to say. What on earth was she talking about?

She was glaring at me, looking like she wanted a fight, but Mum interrupted.

'You've got the wrong girl, love – Vicky can't read or write, never mind send love notes.' And the pub fell silent. I was so ashamed that I couldn't read or write that I looked at the floor with embarrassment. Ironically, my illiteracy saved me this time. It was my first lesson on the consequences of having friendships with pub regulars. I probably had been flirting with this irate woman's husband, but there was definitely no affair. It should've taught me to be more careful but I just carried on regardless. There was a growing recklessness to my behaviour. It was like I didn't care enough about myself to stay out of trouble.

Eventually, Mum and Dad got a flat in Ockenden and we settled for a while. Dad still went off now and again to do some holiday cover at pubs around the area but Mum, Kirsty and I stayed in our new home. Many family friends already lived in Ockenden so fortunately we had people to hang out with. But, as soon as I got settled and began to enjoy the idea of a new home, Mum dropped a bombshell.

'By the way, Vicky,' she said one morning, 'Did I tell you that David is living here with his new girlfriend?'

My heart almost fell to the ground. I was devastated. He'd been out of our lives for so long that I'd got used to him not being there, and now he was around again it took me straight back to square one.

'Oh, nice,' I managed, in a strangled voice, my hard-fought confidence melting away. Mum looked so happy.

'Yeah, it means we can all spend more time together again, like a proper family.'

I wanted to cry. If I could have, I would have. But I hadn't cried for so long it felt like my tear ducts were blocked. My stomach ached with despair all over again.

The first time I saw David again, I felt like my life was on rewind. The old familiar sickness, heaviness and weakness returned. I hated it; I hated him being around again and making me feel so scared. I couldn't understand what his intentions were, so I did everything I could think of to keep Kirsty out of the house so there would be no risk of him seeing her without me being there. I took her for beach-front walks for hours at a time, getting quite fit in the process.

'Are you going to the beach again?' Mum used to laugh.

'Oh, I love the sea air,' I lied. But as weeks passed I noticed that David didn't seem to care about Kirsty. He had always hated babies so thankfully, while Kirsty was still in her nappies, David just didn't want to know. I was so relieved. For the time being, we were safe.

The older David had got, the sleazier he looked. He had a constant lazy grin on his face and, with his blonde floppy hair and glasses, he looked older than his years. There was a twitchy, unpredictable edge to him that made people feel uncomfortable and his knuckles were constantly bust up from the fights he'd picked with his so-called mates. I hated everything about him and always wondered what women saw in him. He was never romantic or affectionate with his girlfriends – if anything, he was quite the opposite – which made me question even more why women were attracted to him. It was as if they wanted to be treated badly. It didn't make sense. David made my skin crawl. Whatever anyone else thought, I knew he was a disgusting pervert and I didn't trust him with anyone.

If it hadn't have been for David, I would have loved being in Ockenden. We lived in a square block of flats with a grassed garden area in the middle and Kirsty and I often sat and played in the communal garden. One day we'd been sitting on the grass for a while when Lisa, the woman from the flat opposite, came over with her little girl. We started talking and hit it off, comparing feeds, teething and sleeping patterns – usual mum talk, I suppose, but something quite new to me. Other teenagers my age seemed to live in a completely different world. As time passed, Lisa and I got more and more friendly and I began to like the fact that, through Kirsty, I had made a new friend. Lisa lived with her boyfriend, Pete. Pete was very skinny, while Lisa was quite curvy, so they looked funny together, but they'd talk to anyone and were very sociable. Both in their twenties, they assumed I was around the same age too. I didn't correct them, and their flat became my regular hideaway. One day, I watched Pete roll a spliff. Seeing my expression, he asked, 'Do you want some, then?' and I didn't hesitate. I remembered how mind-numbingly nice it was last time and it didn't let me down this time either. I felt all my troubles drift away. After that, I was hooked and I often went round to Lisa's flat just to have a smoke with Pete. It was incredibly irresponsible, but having David back in my life really shook me up, and back then I would have tried anything that helped me forget what a horrible mess I was in.

Not long after moving to Ockenden, Mum suggested I go back to school. I hadn't been for years, but Mum thought it was important that I got to grips with some of the basic skills of reading and writing, so she filled in some forms and registered me at the local secondary school. I was really nervous about it. What would my classmates think about a teen mum like me who struggled with reading a cereal box?

I remember walking into the local Ockenden secondary school for the first time and feeling like a total outsider. I'd hated school all my life, and I definitely didn't feel like I needed school now, after everything that had happened.

I was even more worried about being around kids than I was before having Kirsty. I'd had to grow up so fast that I couldn't cope being amongst teenagers my own age. I was terrified that they would judge me, but it also killed me to see the carefree lives they were living. David hadn't just taken away my childhood – he'd made it impossible for me to be a normal teenager too.

When I walked into the classroom, twenty faces stared back at me. I felt a little stronger than I did years earlier though; maybe, because I'd been through so much, I figured nothing could hurt me now. I even stared back at the kids. I would never have done that before. I used to permanently look at the floor. The first few lessons were miserable. I was even further behind than I'd feared, and had no idea what the teachers were going on about. No one offered to be my partner in chemistry lab, so I had to make a three with two girls who talked non-stop about clothes, music and boys, and ignored me as much as possible. When I tried to join in they just shot me pitying looks, and carried straight on. I felt like such a failure. At mid-morning break, I snuck out and went to Pete's. Soon, whenever I was supposed to be at school, I was at Pete's. I got away with it for ages, until the authorities got in touch with Mum.

'Vicky, when are you going to get an education?' she said, exasperated.

'I don't need one. I'm a mum now, and that's all that matters,' I said. I was so naïve that I actually believed it.

'Suit yourself.'

Kirsty started crying so Mum went off to check on her. Looking back, I wish Mum hadn't given in and let me do what I wanted. There was a definite self-destructive streak to my behaviour at the time, and it was about to get worse.

* * *

When I should have been at school making friends my own age, or spending quality time with Kirsty, I was busy getting friendly with a lot of the twenty-somethings that hung around at Pete's place. It was here that I met Helen, David's new girlfriend. I'd been prepared to dislike her – how could anyone decent love my brother? – but she totally won me over. Knowing now what was to happen, it breaks my heart to remember the evenings we spent there, just sitting and chatting and swapping stories. She had a kid too, from a previous relationship. I'd give anything to be able to go back in time and warn her. At the time I tried – I did my best – but it wasn't nearly enough to save her.

My brother's girlfriend was a tall and pretty girl, with long blonde corkscrew curls. Her voice was soft and tender, and she always had time to give me advice about Kirsty or help Lisa out making tea. I often wanted to ask her how she met David and what she saw in him – I was curious, wondering how anyone so lovely could fall for him. But I never did. My voice shook whenever I mentioned David, so I was too scared I'd give something away. Helen was warmer and more open than most of the girls on the estate. She had that friendly glow and everyone loved her. She was a great mum, and used to give me a lot of tips at times when Kirsty was teething and wasn't sleeping all night. She was wonderful, and she deserved a whole lot better than what fate had in store for her.

Because, unfortunately, wherever Helen was David wasn't far behind. I felt any time spent with Helen was rushed, because I was always waiting for David to come round the corner. That was always my signal to leave. I just couldn't spend a single minute in the same room as him. 'You really hate your brother, don't you?' Helen said one day.

'Yeah, he's a nightmare brother. You know what they're like,' I said awkwardly, my mind swimming. Was this my chance to scare her off him? Helen was so sweet; I felt I owed it to her to try. I found it so difficult to find the words: 'Actually, Helen, are you sure he's the right guy for you? I know he's my brother and everything, but he's . . . I mean, you're so great, and maybe you guys aren't . . .'

But she just smiled and cut me off. 'Don't be silly, Vicks. I'm a big girl, and I can look after myself.'

Even when she came round to Pete's with a black eye a few weeks later, Helen insisted that she was fine, that she'd had a stupid accident. Fights weren't unusual in our neck of the woods, so we all pretended to believe her. If only I'd known what would happen, I would have risked everything to get Helen away from David. As it was, I didn't break my silence, and I'm not sure whether I can ever forgive myself for that.

While all this was going on at Pete's, back at home things were falling apart. My parents didn't like my new friends – who were all older and into smoking weed – and it started to drive a wedge between my family and me. Mum didn't like Pete: she thought he was a bad influence. Whenever I asked if I could go to the cinema with him and Lisa, Mum refused, so in the end I lied and said I was taking Ben for a walk. I'd leave the flat at about 2pm and I wouldn't return until 9pm. Mum would be frantic by the time I got back, and always shouted at me when I walked into the house. But I'd walk into my bedroom, slam the door and ignore her. Dad never said anything; he thought I was just going through a phase. Inside I was all messed up – never sure if I was supposed to be acting like an adult, a teenager, or the scared, mixed-up kid I really was.

The arguments between Mum and I grew and grew. We were constantly in a mood with one another after yet another row. One day Mum sent me to the shops to get some milk. I did as I was told but on the way back I lost the change. It was awful, given the sacrifices my parents had made to look after me and Kirsty, but back then I could be pretty careless with other people's money. When I got home I slammed the milk down onto the kitchen worktop and walked off.

'Excuse me, young lady, have you got my change?' Mum asked.

I checked my pocket again and shrugged. 'I don't know what I did with it. Must've fallen out of my pocket. Sorry 'bout that.'

I saw her face fill with rage – she'd had a bad day, and she went ballistic.

'Don't lie to me. Do you think I'm stupid? You've spent it on cigarettes, haven't you?' she shouted.

'There's no need to shout at me, Mum, I told you I don't know where the change went.'

'What's happened to you?' she blazed. 'You'll end up like your brother David. Do you want a life of trouble with the police?'

As soon as Mum brought David into the conversation, I couldn't take it. I began to feel claustrophobic and my head was hurting from her shouting. She wouldn't let me speak; she just kept raging at me. I felt like I was being pushed into a corner. The way I had been feeling, I only needed someone to give me a little push before I completely lost it. I couldn't think clearly and my head was fuzzy. Next minute, without thinking, I ran to my bedroom and opened the window and jumped out. I was two storeys up, but I landed on the grass outside the building. I don't know what came over me. I could've been seriously injured but luckily I only suffered a sprained ankle. My head was all over the place; like it was so full of pent-up emotion and unshed tears that it was ready to explode.

Even though jumping out of a window was completely random and out of control, thinking back it was definitely a cry for help. I was desperate, frustrated, stressed and sad. Mum obviously had no idea what state of mind I was in and thought she was just telling off her wayward daughter, like any mother would. The secret that I had kept had been, bit by bit, eroding my confidence, my self-worth, my relationship with my family and my own sanity. From the outside I might have looked like a rebellious teenager, but inside I was on the verge of a nervous breakdown. Jumping out of the window showed how desperate I was to escape. What I didn't realise then, though, is that there was no escape, nowhere to run to, when your whole life is based on lies.

That was really a turning point in my life. I'd missed so much school by that time that the education welfare officers were in contact with my parents, who were starting to worry about me too. They all concluded it was going to take a miracle to get me to a regular school, so they suggested I went to a boarding school for kids who had difficulties in mainstream schools. At first I thought it was the craziest idea and was scared of leaving Kirsty as, even though David hadn't paid her much attention as a baby, I was terrified that he'd do something as soon as I was out of the way. As far as I was concerned, he was capable of anything. But, at the same time, I had to face facts: I was going off the rails and if I didn't sort myself out I'd ruin both of our lives. I felt so torn.

It was difficult to hide my tears from Mum. 'Why are you so worried about Kirsty?' she asked. 'You know she'll be happy with me while you concentrate on your studies.'

There was silence for a few seconds; I looked at Mum, then looked at the floor. Could I say it? How do I say it? Would it solve everything or make it even worse? Mum just stared at me.

'Vicky, are you listening to me? Kirsty will be fine.' And her firm voice pulled me out of my trance. My moment was gone and Mum walked out of the room. There was nothing else I could do. I had to convince myself that Kirsty would be safe with Mum – that Mum cherished her baby granddaughter even more than she loved her dangerous son.

So, with my mind full of all the dreadful things David might do, I went along with my parents to see a few schools. They were better than I had imagined and some of them even allowed pupils to go home at weekends. The one I liked best was by the sea and had private rooms. The staff seemed nice, so in the end I decided to go for it. It was a chance to get away from everything and hopefully get back on track. I was determined to build a safe, solid future for me and my little girl. But what I wasn't prepared for was for life to take another drastic turn for the worse.

10

True Colours

I left for boarding school on my fourteenth birthday, when Kirsty was just ten months old. Dad dropped me off but as soon as I arrived and unpacked I was uncomfortable. I instantly knew I'd made the wrong decision. I was welcomed by one of the teachers and she tried to be nice, but we didn't connect. She looked harsh and unfriendly – not the type of person a nervous girl wants to see when they arrive somewhere strange. I said goodbye to Dad and, as we hugged, I couldn't let go.

'C'mon now, love,' he said. 'Let go. The lady is waiting for you. You'll be fine. We'll call and you'll make lots of new friends.'

'Yeah, you're right, I'll be fine.' I tried to smile at him, still clutching on to his arm for dear life.

Eventually I let Dad go and watched him drive away. Crying just wasn't my style, but saying goodbye to my little girl and then my lovely father was too much for me and I felt my heart crack.

The teacher took me through the school, pointing out the classrooms and common rooms. It looked like a big old house, with lots of wood and tall ceilings. After the bustle of our terraced house, filled with the sound of Kirsty playing and my mum chatting on the phone, it was very quiet and eerie. I followed the lady around, glancing into bare rooms and down empty echoing corridors. It felt like a prison. For the first time I wondered if I was being sent here as some sort of punishment. Did they somehow know what David had done to me? Did they think it was my fault? Or was this just where they sent girls who got pregnant at twelve years old?

When I was shown to my own room I was relieved to have it to myself, but it wasn't exactly homely. It was old and small and I felt like a caged animal.

'Here you go,' the teacher said. 'Get yourself settled and then come and have a look around when you're ready.'

I nodded at her, but as soon as she left I closed the door and sat on the window ledge and smoked out of the window to calm my nerves. I stayed in my room for hours, staring into the sky. While I was in my daze one of the teachers came into the room and caught me smoking. I was shouted at on my first day and, after that, teachers kept a constant eye on me. They'd decided I was bad girl, a troublemaker, and that was that.

I didn't socialise or meet anyone that night. I just wanted to pretend I wasn't there. I could hear girls giggling and talking on the landing, but I was too scared to go out there. My experiences with teenage schoolgirls hadn't been great, and I didn't want to be ignored, teased or humiliated by a whole new lot of them. It's a very lonely feeling to sit on your own and hear the laughter and happiness of friends being reunited after the holidays. Part of me ached to slip outside and join them, and I even jumped up and got as far as the door at one stage before slumping back down on the bed. I was too proud to risk being rejected again, and I had no idea what I would say if they asked me about my family. It seemed safer to sit on my own in the darkness, trying not to listen to their raucous voices.

The next day was no different. I was like a shy little child again, retreating into my shell. The teachers had a lot of control over us all and it was hard for someone like me, who had been used to having my own way, to be disciplined. Being controlled so much made me feel really claustrophobic. I couldn't go out when I wanted, couldn't eat when I wanted, couldn't have a walk or a talk when I wanted – everything was restricted. I'd been used to doing things my way and to being a mother with adult responsibilities, and now I was like a dog on a short lead. I didn't like being controlled. It made me feel like I was that little girl again, the one that David raped.

As I got used to the monotonous routine and the endless rules, I tried to make friends with some of the quieter girls. We were all in the same boat, after all, and I had promised my dad that I'd make the best of it. In the queue for lunch one day, I pointed to the grey mashed potato that the dinner ladies were scooping out.

'Looks like someone's already eaten it and thrown it back up again.'

The brunette girl in front of me rolled her eyes and moved away from me. The one behind, who I'd been teamed up with last week for netball practice, spoke up.

'Look, I'm not being funny, but I'd stay away from Karen and her mates if I were you. They already think you're a bit weird.'

'Oh, right,' I said, deflated. I was so unused to spending time with other teenage girls that they were like an alien breed to me, with their cliques and hierarchies. I just didn't know how to interact with them. And the girls at this school seemed particularly edgy – perhaps because lots of them had been in trouble with the authorities before being sent here. Maybe if I found out more about how my

year group worked, I would do better at making friends?
I turned round to ask my neighbour some more about the
popular clique, but she'd already gone off to sit with her
own friends. Trying to look like I didn't care, I took my
unappetising plate of sausage and mash and sat down on
an empty table in a corner of the noisy room.

As the weeks passed, the situation didn't really improve
and I felt very alone. We were allowed to go home at
weekends, but it was so far away from home that Dad
couldn't afford the petrol money to keep driving me back
and forth. Instead they called often. Sometimes Dad was
working in a pub, so I wouldn't always get to speak to him,
but Mum would fill me in on the news. 'Kirsty is talking a
lot more,' she'd tell me. 'She was almost on top of Ben the
other day, but the dopey fool just let her do whatever she
wanted to him. You should have seen it.' I was desperate
for details, but it was so hard hearing about home.

'Oh, Mum, please can I come back? I miss you guys and
Kirsty so much,' I'd beg.

She'd sigh down the phone. 'You can't. You know you
have to stay. You've missed so much school. You have to
finish it, for Kirsty's sake, if not for your own.' It wasn't
what I wanted to hear, but I had no choice. Whenever Dad
came on the phone, though, he was so lovely.

'I'd come and get you if I could but you know the
authorities would only catch up with you in the end,' he'd
say. 'Just count down the days until the holidays – it won't
be long.'

Good old Dad, always making me feel better.

I also got a few letters from them. Usually I tried to be
up-beat when I wrote back but one day, after a girl tried
to start a fight with me in the changing rooms, I couldn't
pretend any more. I smuggled one out saying: 'I hate it

here. Get me out!' Mum said that Dad was really quiet for a few days after they got that letter.

I had been at the school for just over a month and was finally feeling more settled when I got a phone call from Mum which changed everything. She'd never called so late before so I knew something was wrong.

'I've got some bad news,' she said.

Hot dread surged through my body. Please let nothing have happened to Kirsty! I should never have left her! Mum's voice cut through my panic.

'David's been arrested . . . he's killed Helen.'

As I digested the news, I couldn't speak. Lovely, kind Helen who'd shown me how to take care of Kirsty, dead? But she was so vibrant and young and lovely. There must be some mistake . . . I just couldn't take it in.

'Vicky? Are you there?'

I didn't know what to say. Mum went on to explain the situation in more detail but I had already switched off – my mind had travelled to a place where there was no David and he didn't exist. Eventually, I told Mum I had to go; I couldn't listen to her and my head was spinning. I hung-up without properly finding out what had happened. All I knew was that the brother who had destroyed my childhood had now killed a young woman with her whole life ahead of her. I didn't think I could hate David any more than I already did. I was wrong.

As I walked back to my room, I tried to get my head around the situation. I'd never felt such a mix of emotions in all my life. I was devastated that Helen was dead. She was beautiful and had been so sweet to me. How must her family feel? What about her little boy, who had just lost his mummy? I also felt agonisingly guilty. Yes, it was

David who killed Helen. But what if I had told someone about him raping me? She'd never have trusted him then. I could've saved her. I had been the only person who really knew David. If I had been able to tell someone my terrible secret, he could have been locked up years earlier. So many conflicting thoughts were rushing through my head. I struggled to breathe as I tried to take in the news.

I wanted to go straight back to my room to be alone, but I was instantly smothered by all the teachers fussing around me. 'Are you OK, Vicky? Come and talk to us, we can help,' they kept saying. I wanted to scream at them: 'Leave me alone!' I'd never felt so trapped. They thought I would feel better if I spoke about what had happened – and maybe they were right. But I was fourteen years old, completely devastated, and I just wanted to be alone. I'd been so used to dealing with my own problems in my own way; I found it impossible to put my feelings into words. I just wanted everyone to leave me alone and let me deal with things like I'd been used to.

I spent the night locked in my room, thinking. The following day I was supposed to go on a sports activity day the school had arranged weeks earlier, but I didn't want to go.

'Just leave me here, I'm sorry, but I don't think I can take it today,' I said. But the teachers wouldn't take no for an answer.

'It'd be good for you to get out,' my form mistress said, standing in the doorway with her hands on her hips.

In the end I pushed them out of my room and moved my chest of drawers in front of the door to keep them out. I sat in my room for hours, smoking, thinking about Helen and going over and over what David had done to her.

Hours passed, and eventually I realised the place was silent. I couldn't hear a thing. I moved the drawers away from the door and peeked through a crack. No one was there. Instinctively I decided to run, to get the hell away from all these prying people. Without thinking things through, I grabbed a bag and bolted out the door.

As we were rarely allowed off school premises I had no idea where I was going, but I'd heard that the town centre was only ten minutes away so I followed my feet to the seafront. It felt so good just to be out of that place where every time I breathed I seemed to be breaking a rule or annoying one of the popular girls. I found it really hard to cope with the constant rejection. It was better to be alone than to be lonely in that crowded place.

When I got into town I just sat on a bench and let all my troubles drift away on the sea breeze. Seeing me staring into space, a guy approached me. I shrank back, wondering what he was after, but he seemed like a friendly young guy so I nodded when he asked if he could sit down.

'So, what are you doing here, then?' he asked. The last thing I wanted was for him to call the police so I told him I'd fallen out with my parents. He looked hard at me but nodded slowly. I couldn't help noticing how good-looking he was.

'Got anywhere to sleep tonight?'

'Haven't really thought about it.' As I said it, I realised that it must be getting pretty late.

'Look, why don't we see if my parents will let you stay in the spare room? I'm sure it won't be a problem.'

I paused. He seemed kind and trustworthy, but I had already found out first-hand how appearances could be deceptive. But what choice did I have? The thought of going back to school and being forced to talk about David made me feel sick. The streets were getting less and less busy, and I hadn't really thought through how dangerous it would be for a young girl to spend the night alone in a park or shop doorway.

'OK then.'

I followed the lad home like a stray puppy. It was such a relief when he took me to the suburban street where he lived, just like he'd promised. All the way back I'd been trying not to think about what the consequences of putting all my trust in a strange man might be.

That night I ended up sleeping under a bush near his parents' house. Turns out his parents weren't such good Samaritans after all, and they weren't too keen on letting me stay in the house. Thankfully, it was summer so it wasn't too cold, but it was raining and so I woke up soaked to the skin and shivering. The bush barely covered my body. Looking back, I'm horrified at the way I put myself in so much danger, sleeping on the dirt like an animal. At the time though, I was so mixed up that I didn't feel like I deserved any better.

The next day I waited for the guy to come out, with no clue what to do or where to go next.

'Vicky, you can't sleep rough like this,' he said. 'I think there's a squat not far from here, where they might let you stay.'

'A squat? Do you know them?' I asked. There had been some squatters in some of the council flats near us and Dad had always warned me to have nothing to do with them.

'Well, I've seen them around.' He seemed to be losing patience. 'Look, Vicky, you can't live in my front garden!' He was right, and I knew he was trying to help me, but I was really scared about how these strangers would react when I turned up out of the blue.

'Nothing . . . nothing goes on there, does it?' I stuttered, but he was already walking away. My self-preservation instincts were at an all-time low so I just followed quietly, too tired to ask any more questions.

The squat was big, ramshackle and looked unwelcoming. My friend had to bang on the door for five minutes before it flung open and a bedraggled woman in her thirties asked us what we were after. I wanted to turn and run. This was such a big mistake. But as soon as we'd explained the situation, she smiled and welcomed me warmly.

'Hello love, come in, make yourself at home.'

She looked a bit scruffy but seemed friendly. Her partner was the same age as her and he motioned for me to come in. I said goodbye to the guy who had helped me and stepped inside. I was so naïve that I didn't even stop and think about possible dangers. While still a child I'd been attacked in my own bed, so I suppose on some level I believed that it didn't matter where I was. Nowhere was safe.

This time I was lucky, however. I said I was seventeen and the squatters gave me a bed without asking any more questions. There were sixteen people altogether, but it was nothing like the typical squats I'd heard about. As I walked through the house I kept bumping into lots of different people who would smile and say hi to me. I guess I wasn't the only one running away from something I couldn't face, but they were much kinder and more friendly than most 'respectable' people I'd met. There were no drug needles lying around the place, or people sleeping in their own dirt for days. It was just like a normal home, albeit a bit cramped. That night they made me dinner – beans on toast – and I listened to the rest of them chat about their lives. It was so good to stay quiet and just listen, and it distracted me from obsessing over Helen and David.

Eventually I headed to bed in a room I shared with a few people. I hadn't got much sleep under the bush the night before, so I fell asleep quickly. Despite being surrounded by strange bodies I felt totally safe, and had the best night's sleep I'd had since I left home.

When I got up the following morning though, the memory of what David had done to Helen hit me like a kick in the chest. I could never go back. The guilt and disgust had snapped me in half. If I somehow managed to stay with these kind people, then maybe I could become someone else. Someone whose life wasn't such a mess. I decided to change my appearance. Part of me wanted to get home, of course, to be with my parents and, most importantly, with Kirsty, but I just couldn't face the truth of what David had done and I was also terrified of being sent back to school. So I borrowed some hair dye and coloured my hair bright red, and shaved the sides. I ended up looking like a proper 80s punk. Looking back I can't help but laugh. But at the time I thought I looked brilliant and that it was a perfect disguise. I looked much tougher, and inside I felt tougher too. I looked like a girl no one could hurt.

As soon as I was sure I didn't look like the old Vicky, I headed back into town. I walked and walked, and felt so free. I came across a funfair and got friendly with some of the workers. 'Can I have a job?' I asked, after a few hours of flirting.

That night I helped out on the Waltzers. In a way I created a new life for myself in the space of just a few days. I got myself the job at the fair and went home to a bunch of lovely people and had food, even though it was usually tinned hot dogs and baked beans all the time. They were fantastically generous, and the longer I was there, the easier it was to forget the old vulnerable, mixed-up Vicky and all her problems. I should have known that it couldn't have lasted for long.

I was walking along the seafront one afternoon, after I'd been in the squat for about five days, when I saw a policewoman head straight for me holding some posters. I froze. 'Do I run or pretend to be calm?' I thought. I was terrified the police were looking for me and that she'd recognise me. My heart was racing as she drew nearer.

'Excuse me, young lady, do you recognise the girl in this photo?' the officer asked.

Staring back at me was a school photo of myself. I thought it was a joke, but then I realised the officer didn't recognise me.

'Erm, no, sorry, I haven't seen her,' I said.

'If you do, can you go down to the station? She's run away and her family is very worried,' she added, and left.

Part of me felt very relieved – like I'd just got away with something – but I also felt really guilty. I didn't want to put my parents through so much grief on top of everything else and I was missing Kirsty. Most of all, though, I was scared. I wasn't thinking straight and all I could focus on was putting distance between me and David. I have to admit that I was also enjoying my newfound freedom – it was such an escape from people interfering or judging me. No one knew me here and it felt like a fresh start, away from my messed-up old life.

But my luck was running out. Another few days passed and I was increasingly convinced that someone was going to find me. My escape had been too easy to be true. Before my shift at the fair that night I sat under the pier on some stones and looked out to the sea with only my thoughts for company. I'd been sitting there for hours when I saw my squatter friends approach. I just knew my time was up.

'Vicky, we've seen your photo on the news,' the oldest lad said. My heart sank and I carried on looking out to sea. 'C'mon, we're taking you to the police.'

I didn't put up a fight; I knew it was time. I'd been thinking too much about Kirsty and how I couldn't desert her. I had to go home; I had my daughter to protect. The thought of leaving David any chance to get near her made my skin turn cold. I missed my little girl's big hugs, and I worried that being so far away from Kirsty made her vulnerable.

As soon as I got to the station I said my goodbyes to my new friends and they left. I stood at the station reception and took a deep breath.

'My family has been looking for me,' I told the officer. I was taken to a cell and left there for the night. I think they thought I was trouble and, as I didn't look that young, they just left me in the cell. It was one of the worst nights of my life. David had killed Helen and now I was sleeping in a cell like a prisoner!

When Mum finally arrived I was surprised how pleased I was to see her.

'Oh my God, Vicky, what have you done to your hair?' she squealed, and we laughed, getting rid of the awkwardness. Thankfully no one asked any questions and I wasn't forced to reveal anything of the last ten days. My family were never big on talking through their problems. On the way home I sat in the car in silence, thinking about what I was about to face when I got home. I remembered the phone call – about David and Helen. How was life going to pan out from here?

As soon as I walked through the door a crowd of people came running towards me, hugging and kissing me. I started crying because I was so happy to be home and to know that David was out of the way. My entire body was engulfed in relief: relief that I had my family to myself; relief that David wasn't going to be a dark cloud overshadowing everything; and relief that Kirsty and I would finally be safe.

'Oh, girl, where have you been?' Dad said, hugging me as tight as ever and kissing me all over my head.

'I'm sorry Dad,' I sobbed. I couldn't believe I'd put them through all that. I hugged Kirsty to my body and let the tears flow for once.

The following day, members from the education department showed up and I ran to my bedroom and locked myself inside. They tried to send me back to the boarding school, but I refused to come out of the room. I think it convinced them how strongly I felt about it and eventually they left me alone, agreeing with Mum that a home tutor would be best. I was overjoyed. Now I was back with Kirsty, I couldn't stand the thought of not being around to protect her.

Over the next few weeks, David's arrest and imprisonment became the focus of daily life.

Little by little the facts of Helen's killing came out, and what I heard sickened me to the core. That night, David had spent the evening with Helen at her flat while her child was asleep. They'd had an argument which had started out as an angry exchange of words, but had got more and more violent as David's physical aggression spun out of control. Knowing David, I'm sure that wasn't the first time he had hurt her. But this time he didn't know when to stop. In a fit of rage, David ended up grabbing Helen around her neck and suffocating her. Seeing what he had done, he dragged her dead body back onto the sofa and sat with her all night. The next morning he went to see Mum and told her what had happened. Mum immediately called the police. She told me that she'd barely been able to take in what he said, but had just picked up the phone, dialled 999, and said very calmly: 'I need a police officer. My son has just told me he's killed his girlfriend.' David claimed it was an accident, but he was arrested and charged with murder.

I stayed in the house with Kirsty while Mum and Dad went back and forth to the police station, lawyer's office and to see David in prison. They were so worried and I had to pretend to be too, but deep down all I did was pray he'd get locked up for life. If only Mum and Dad had known what I was really thinking. I felt sorry for them, in some ways, because they were genuinely concerned for their son, thinking he wasn't evil enough to deliberately kill someone. My feelings were so confused. Seeing how destroyed they were by the accusations against my brother, I knew there was no way that I could say anything to make the situation worse. The truth would destroy my family and now they needed me more than ever. As much as it hurt me, I had to be strong and keep my silence.

As if things weren't bad enough for Mum and Dad, the entire neighbourhood seemed to turn against us. We had bricks and planks of wood thrown through our windows. Neighbours called us 'murdering scum' to our faces. Mum was walking through town one day and one of Helen's sisters appeared in front of her. Mum didn't know where to look or what to say, but before she had the chance to do anything Helen's sister spat in her face. It was awful. Don't get me wrong, though – I don't blame Helen's family for being so sad and angry, as any family would react in the same way. If only they'd known how I hated David as much as they did!

Our police liaison officers kept in touch and constantly advised us to keep out of Helen's family's way. We tried – the last thing we wanted to do was make life even harder for them – but in the end it got so difficult we had to move.

We got a new council house down the road in Purfleet. I was quite sad to leave Ockenden because I'd made some good friends and I liked the area. I was so angry with David that we had to leave – even when he was in prison he was still ruining our lives. It was so unfair that the whole family were tainted by his crime. I hated him so much that it got harder and harder to keep my feelings to myself. But every time the feelings resurfaced and I almost opened my mouth to tell, something always stopped me. The image of my dad's shocked and sad face would engulf my mind whenever I thought about telling him. It felt an impossible subject to discuss – completely taboo. It was like someone had locked a box of dark poisonous secrets inside me. I just never had the key to open it and, to be honest, even I was scared of what was inside.

The new house was a small maisonette on an old estate built during the Second World War. With three adults and a baby, it was quite a squeeze. But it was in Purfleet that I started my home tutoring. I had a teacher come round for an hour once a week and most of that time was spent chatting and drinking tea – nice, but a bit pointless. It was like everyone had given up on me. By fourteen I could just about write my name – another shameful secret to add to my stash. Yet, in our rough and downtrodden world, school just wasn't important. With David's trial on everyone's lips, it was all I could do just to make it through each day.

David's trial had been set for the following February and he was to remain in custody until that time. Mum was distraught because she believed David when he'd said that Helen's death was an accident, as she could never think ill of her golden boy. But I was just glad he was no longer around – it was such a weight off my mind. 'I'm off to see David tomorrow, are you coming?' Mum often asked. I always made my excuses.

'I'm busy Mum,' I lied. 'Anyway, David isn't bothered about seeing me.'

But Mum looked devastated. 'He needs us Vicky, he needs his family around him,' she'd say, her voice quivering. 'I'm worried about him.'

Seeing her so upset tore me apart. I wanted to tell her to shut up, that he wasn't worth a minute's worry. I felt my blood rising to boiling point the more she went on. It's the most frustrating thing in the world listening to someone defending a person you know to be evil and dishonest.

'Mum, he's a big boy,' I managed in the end, before walking out. But in my head I continued: 'And he doesn't deserve your love.' I hated myself for being so weak, but I couldn't make things worse for my family. They were so close to breaking point and I didn't see how they could have survived another shock.

Things at home were so fraught that I ended up spending as much time as possible out and about, making new friends. I jumped from one boyfriend to the next, hoping one would give me what I wanted, and somehow be my knight in shining armour. But while I was a hopeless romantic inside, outside I made sure I never seemed vulnerable. As I got older and more confident, I got a lot tougher. I think I'd been through so much that I wasn't scared of anything or anyone. I genuinely felt that I had already been at rock bottom so no one could hurt me that much again. Throughout my life, David is the only person I've ever been scared of; after him there was nothing else anyone could throw at me. So, if I faced any bullies, gangs, or rough people on the estates, I gave as good as I got. In the end, people were scared of me! I'm not saying I was proud of myself, but it was such a relief to not always be the victim.

This was a time in my life when I started to wonder what had made David the way he was. The way my life had panned out – constant disruption, rape, bullying, early motherhood – had certainly changed me. Maybe David could say the same; maybe he felt his surroundings made him who he is? I hated to think that there was any similarity between us: he was a violent sexual predator, and I was a shy little girl who had to grow up much too fast. But making the connection between my defensiveness and David's aggression made me even more determined to never be like him, and to only use my hard-won toughness to defend myself and the people I loved. It would have been easy to let all the bitterness and hatred spill over into aggression, but I was determined that I would never hurt people the way David did, never destroy someone weaker and more vulnerable than me.

However, I didn't have any qualms about hurting myself. I'd already been using cannabis as a form of escapism for years, but my new friends were also into alcohol and harder drugs. While my parents were obsessed with the details of my brother's trial, I was willing to try anything to help me forget. By now I didn't really act like a mother at all and Kirsty turned to Mum for everything. Looking back, I can't believe how screwed up my priorities were, but there was a part of me that seemed hell-bent on self-destruction.

One night, I got so drunk I collapsed and slept on the pavement in town. All I remember is being woken by two police officers dragging me to my feet. I didn't know who they were or what they wanted; I immediately thought the worst and began defending myself. Being grabbed while I was sleeping was far too close to what David did to me, and I ended up flailing my arms wildly and breaking the nose of one of the officers. I was in a lot of trouble because of that and so they took me to the station and held me in a cell overnight. Just like my brother, I had lashed out. And, just like him, I was locked up in a prison cell. The alcohol got me through the night, but, when I woke up, sober and shaking, I was pretty terrified. I wondered what was going to happen to me, but I'd heard that minors weren't meant to stay in custody. Growing up with a criminal brother taught you stuff like that. Sure enough, by the morning, the officers had realised that I was only fourteen and panicked, sending me home.

I'd been on the social services' 'at risk register' since giving birth to Kirsty, so the police called them and they picked me up from the station. When we got back home Dad just looked at me like I'd let him down. Mum was cheery with the social workers, but then started lecturing me about being a young lady. I'm ashamed to say that I didn't listen. If they couldn't see what David was really like, even after he killed Helen, how dare they try and tell me how to live my life?

The night in the cells didn't teach me anything. One night, soon after, I was out with some other boys and got drunk on pints of snakebite. A guy I liked was talking to another woman and I got so paranoid and jealous that I ended up drinking much more than I meant to. I was only fourteen, but I was trying to match drinks with all the grown men. I was out of control, and it could have turned into a really nasty situation, but one of the lads took pity on me and dropped me off at home in the early hours of the morning. I was too drunk and ill to go inside, so instead I collapsed on the doorstep. I remember hearing bottles banging together and the next minute I came face to face with the milkman. I must have given him a heart attack!

'Oh, sorry love, are you all right?' he asked, stepping round my body.

Feeling humiliated, I dragged myself up and into the house. My dad was sitting in the kitchen. I'd never seen him look so angry.

'Where have you been? Do you know how worried your mother and I have been?' he began, his voice getting louder and louder.

I backed away towards my room, wanting to collapse on my bed. 'I'm sorry Dad,' I managed. Usually my dad would have let me get away, but this time he stopped me from going anywhere and sat me down.

'What are you doing to yourself? There's all sorts of stories going round. They say you're just a whore. Look at you . . . you're a disgrace,' he shouted. I felt distraught seeing the disgust on his face. I'd obviously scared him to death being out all night, not knowing what had happened to me. He even looked like he might hit me, so I ran upstairs. It really upset me seeing Dad that way with me. I thought he would always be on my side but I'd obviously pushed him too far. I wasn't his little princess any more. I ran upstairs and cried my eyes out.

That day I decided that something had to change. I didn't want to be around people who were a bad influence any more, and I had to quit the drinking and drugs. I definitely didn't want to ever see Dad lose his temper like that with me again. The thought of losing his support terrified me. He was the only person who had ever really loved me as I was, and I couldn't afford to lose him.

11

Trial and Reappearance

As David's court case loomed my life span further and further out of control. Looking back, I see how I was losing my grip because I was so petrified of the outcome. What if he walked free?

I didn't go to the trial at Chelmsford Crown Court; I just made my excuses and managed to avoid it. Mum thought she understood, assuming it'd be too hard for me to see my brother in the docks. She saw my reluctance as a sign that I loved him, despite our mutual coldness.

'You look after Kirsty, then,' she said. 'David will understand.'

In a way she was right. As much as I hated David, in a strange way he was the only one who understood exactly how I felt about him. While everyone else assumed that, deep down, we loved each other, only my brother and I knew that our relationship was built on fear and intimidation, pain and secrecy.

David's trial lasted four long days. Every day Mum dragged herself to court sobbing, hoping that I'd go with her, and then eventually leaving me with Kirsty. Every night she came home and updated me. I felt sorry for her because she was suffering so much, but my hatred for David was far more powerful, although I tried to hide my feelings of frustration and disgust in front of Mum.

'How was he?' I'd mutter.

'He looked distraught,' Mum would whisper under her breath. 'He's just not coping and I'm worried for him. Please see him Vicky.'

I was running out of excuses by then and I would start to sweat as I looked at my poor, vulnerable Mum, knowing that she couldn't handle any more harsh truths about her son. So, instead, I'd fish for an excuse.

'But I've got Kirsty, Mum – she's my priority. David will cope.'

I lied again and again. My entire life was a lie. I sometimes worried that I'd become such a good actress that I wouldn't even know who I was any more. In that way, I reminded myself of Helen – pretending everything was OK, and that David was a perfectly nice guy. The thought made my blood run cold.

Mum had always been there for David; she never faltered. She was defending him with all her might, even though he was accused of killing someone. I sometimes wondered whether she would ever realise the type of man he really was. She was even a witness for the defence and had to speak about him in front of a jury and tell them how he ran to her on the morning after Helen died and what she had done next. He was found guilty of manslaughter and was sentenced to eight years in prison. Helen's family cheered in the gallery as security kept them away from Mum and the rest of the family.

When Mum told me the verdict I wanted to cheer too. The relief felt like someone had just loosened a belt round my stomach – for the first time in years, my body could relax. The knot of pain, anger and fear finally started to untangle and I was thrilled that he was going to be out of our lives for so long. I was only fourteen then, so eight years seemed like an eternity. Mum, however, was devastated. She cried for days, hardly leaving her room. Dad tried to comfort her but nothing worked. Seeing her waste so many tears on my brother was hard. Sometimes I wanted to tell her my secret and force her to see that she didn't need to suffer for David's sake. It would have been selfish though. At that point, every bad word about David was a slap across Mum's face, and I couldn't bring myself to subject her to more torment.

As soon as the case was over, David requested an appeal. Mum had said he was planning to, but I didn't think he would – how would he have the nerve? I hoped that while he was locked up he'd reflect on all the bad things he'd done and feel some glimmer of remorse. I should have known David better than that.

Three months later his appeal was heard at the Old Bailey, in London. This time I wanted to go along.

'Oh, Vicky, I'm so glad you've seen the light. David will be so happy to see you there,' Mum said. But I wasn't going for David. I wasn't even going for Mum. I was going for me, because I wanted to see David's cocky face crumble when his appeal was refused. I wanted to see him in the dock and I wanted him to see me staring straight at him as I sat in the gallery.

When I saw my brother walk into the dock, though, my heart started beating fast. Mum was holding my hand and she must've felt the beat from my pulse.

'Are you OK?' she asked. 'I know it's hard.'

But really my heart was beating with rage – every time I saw him it was the same, and it never got easier. Thankfully David didn't look up once and while I could see Mum was terrified for him, I didn't feel anything but hate. I wanted him to rot in jail, where he couldn't hurt anyone else.

Turns out, the devil really does look after his own. After just a few minutes David's sentence was reduced by two years. My heart almost collapsed. The judge concluded that, because the conviction was manslaughter and not murder, the initial sentence was too harsh. David's face was pure elation and I was completely gutted. Mum was beaming.

'Six years sounds better than eight, doesn't it, love?'

'It does, Mum. Much shorter.' I said, trying to keep the bitterness out of my voice.

'And the lawyers think it might be four, if he stays out of trouble.'

'Really?' My head shot up. I hadn't even thought of that.

'Yes, Vicks, so there's no need to have that sad look on your face. Your brother will be out and about and playing with his little niece before you even know it.'

My blood ran cold. She gave me one of her rare hugs. It was all too much for me. Despite all my good intentions I went home and rolled myself a joint. Quickly my mind melted and everything felt numb again.

Over the next couple of years, I smoked more and more – some days between thirty and forty joints a day. My mind was continuously numb, and I suppose I liked it that way. Looking back, I can admit I was an addict. I'd experienced the world through a haze of smoke since I was thirteen, so it felt natural. I needed to block things out more than ever, because, even though David was out of the picture for a few years, what he had done to me hadn't gone away. Nightmares of those nights still plagued me, and images of his face still dominated my mind. I couldn't forget everything that had happened. I found that I'd been kidding myself when I'd thought that having David locked up would make everything OK. Wherever David was, he would always be in my head, haunting me like a living ghost.

It wasn't just my brother who turned me into a drug addict, though. In the run-down estates that I had grown up in, it wasn't normal to have ambitions or to want to get an education and do well. Most people drank themselves silly on alcohol or smoked themselves clueless on cannabis, or other, harder drugs. Of course, some didn't, but as a messed-up teenage mum, I wasn't strong enough to fight against the tide. To my troubled mind, cannabis seemed like the only thing that kept me sane, but the knock-on effect was that it also stopped me seeing things in a normal way. It was a vicious cycle. I was terrified about ending up like my brother, but I had no idea how to get out of it.

It probably wasn't a coincidence that the more drugs I took, the more my relationship with my mother deteriorated. There was part of me that found it hard to forget how completely she'd sided with David, and I couldn't stand her telling me what to do.

One day Mum and I had a stupid row about me coming back late. Rather than stay and sort it out like an adult, I put Kirsty in her pushchair, hooked Ben up to his lead and went for a walk. We were gone for hours, sitting on steps, swinging in the park. My little girl was getting bigger, and it was great to spend some time with her, but I knew that wasn't why I'd taken her out. On some level, I wanted to punish Mum – to hurt her. It worked. When we eventually got home Mum was almost in tears.

'Don't you ever do that again! How can you just take Kirsty like that?' she screamed. I walked away, pulling a face, but Mum's hand came out of nowhere and slapped me. For a few seconds I stood there, staring at her. Then I hit her right back. To this day I don't know how I could have raised my hand to my own mother, but all sense of reason had left my mind. Years of anger, frustration and jealousy came pouring out, and Mum and I ended up having a physical fight in our front room. If it hadn't been so awful, it might have been funny. We fell on the floor, tumbled over the sofa; ornaments went flying across the room. For the first time in my life I really wanted to hurt my mother, to punish her for not protecting me, for not seeing through David's lies. Neither of us wanted to back down but, eventually, we stopped, too bruised to carry on.

Later that evening, people were staring at us on the bus. Mum and I hadn't spoken to each other for a few hours by that stage, but next minute we caught one another's eye and we started laughing. All the poison seeped away. We had black eyes, scratches, sprained wrists and bruises.

'We look like we've been in ten rounds with Tyson,' Mum laughed, and I grabbed her hand and didn't let it go.

Once more, though, my sense of shame and remorse didn't last. I was out of control. Not even my Mum could help me, and Dad was busy working, making sure we had money. In quieter moments even I could see I was getting worse. It wasn't just the drugs. I was so desperate for someone to love me that all sense of natural preservation left me. It was a dangerous frame of mind for anyone to be in, never mind a vulnerable teenager with a damaged past.

When I was seventeen, I met Mark. He was ten years older than me but we got on really well. He lived around the corner from me and we had friends in common. Mark was tall with sandy hair, and he was popular with the younger lads. I was flattered that he was interested in me, and was prepared to do whatever it took to keep things that way. But before long the same old pattern emerged: I got very attached very quickly and imagined he was going to be the man I'd spend the rest of my life with. I genuinely thought he was my chance at a happy-ever-after. He was friendly, secure and seemed kind. But, of course, for me, the only way I knew to keep a man interested was to sleep with him. At first it seemed to work, but, after two months together I found out I was pregnant. I was in shock at first; part angry with myself, part scared, because I knew I hadn't been a good mum to Kirsty and that I'd been irresponsible for the last couple of years. How was I going to cope with another child? Why would I be any better? Another part of me was convinced it was different this time though. I wasn't a scared little girl who didn't know what was happening to her any more, and this time my romantic fantasies were working overtime. I wanted a family now, to have Mark by my side and create a loving home. I started to believe this was an opportunity to do just that.

The rest of the family were dismissive.

'This one will end up just like Kirsty,' Aunt Chris said.

'What do you mean?' I snapped at her.

'There's nothing wrong with Kirsty,' Dad put in mildly.

'No, but you haven't exactly been a model mother, have you?' Mum pointed out. 'I've been doing most of the work.'

'Well, I'm still not going to have an abortion,' I said, standing my ground for once. 'Me and Mark will do things properly this time.'

As was often the case, it didn't work out quite like I'd planned.

When I told Mark the news, I was hoping he'd be excited for us. Instead he ended up throwing an ashtray across the room in anger and frustration. In that moment he reminded me of David, losing his rag and lashing out. That was the only sign I needed. I didn't want my child to be around a father like that. I wanted this baby and I wanted to be a proper mum. Little Kirsty was thrown at me when my head was filled with hatred and fear, but this time I knew I was a lot stronger. Whatever my hopes and dreams were, my children had to be the most important people in my life. I'd been so desperate for affection that my priorities had got screwed up, and I was determined that that'd never happen again.

Mark and I stayed in touch throughout the pregnancy, however, and became friends. Plus, this pregnancy was so different from the first. I loved having a baby inside of me and every kick and movement was exciting and emotional at the same time. I loved Kirsty with all my heart, but it was a joy to be carrying a child who wasn't conceived in such terrible circumstances.

I was seventeen, pregnant with my second child, and single again. While my romantic dreams had come to nothing, David's love life just got better and better. Despite being locked up for killing Helen, he was now getting married. When I heard the news I had to sit down as my legs were shaking so much. Turns out that, when my brother was initially convicted, it was reported in the local newspaper and one of his school girlfriends, Nicola, read it and got in touch with him. They wrote to one another for ages and then she started visiting him. When I found out they were getting married I didn't know whether to laugh or cry. Part of me was sick at the thought of him finding happiness while I was alone again, but another part of me thought it was ridiculous – how could Nicola be so naïve? He was in prison for manslaughter!

The last thing I wanted to do in my condition was to see David, but there was no way I was going to get out of the wedding. All the excuses I dreamed up couldn't convince Mum and Dad this time. In their eyes, it was my brother's wedding – the most important day of his life – so why wouldn't I want to go? In the run up to the big day my mum kept trying to get me involved, talking about Nicola's dress, and what I should wear. I know she was trying to get me excited, but she only succeeded in making me dread it even more. What a ridiculous charade – pretending to celebrate the wedding of the man who'd raped me and caused the death of my friend. Part of me wanted to use the silence in the register office to make an announcement. I had vicious fantasies about turning the best day of my tormentor's life into his worst.

But, however it played out in my mind, in reality I was terrified to be in the same room with him after so long, and the most important thing for me was to just stay as far away from him as possible. Thankfully when I asked Mark if he'd accompany me, he agreed.

'Thanks. Just don't leave me – stay by my side all day. I can't stand family celebrations,' I lied. I needed all the protection I could get.

David had done almost three years of his sentence when they let him out for the day to get married. It was 1992, and there were about twenty other family members at Ely register office. The morning of the wedding I tried a few more times to get out of going.

'I don't feel well, Mum, and Kirsty has got a temperature,' I said to Mum. 'I don't want to spoil the day by giving anyone an infection.'

'Don't worry, Vicks, I'll keep an eye on you both,' she said. She was so happy about David's marriage that she couldn't stop smiling. She kept saying that maybe the wedding was the fresh start he needed. I wanted to scream.

'I really don't mind staying here . . .'

With that she fixed me with a hard look. 'Vicky, after everything your brother's been through, there is no way that we're letting him down on his big day. Jesus, Vicks, what did he ever do to you?'

If only she knew. But the dread of seeing David had exhausted me so much that I nodded dully and went to get my shoes. Good little Vicky, doing what she was told. Keeping her mouth shut.

I stayed with Mark all day, clinging to him like a limpet. I'm sure he must have been confused by my behaviour, but he was a great support and I barely saw David at all. My brother played the 'in-love groom' role so well that he had eyes for no one else in the room but Nicola. I barely knew the bride, but I felt sick with worry for her. What would stop David hurting her too? All day I toyed with the idea of saying something, dropping some hint in order to have the new bride on her guard. But she already knew he was a convicted killer – what else could I say? In the end, I stayed in the corner with Mark and, as soon as I could, we left. After the ceremony, the guards took David back to prison and I could breathe again.

Just a few weeks later, I went into labour, on 30 March 1992. Dad drove me to hospital, and Mark waited outside while Mum held my hand in the labour ward. Considering how young I was when I had Kirsty, and the mess she made of my body, this birth was surprisingly easy. After the trauma and tearing of the first birth, this baby virtually plopped out.

I had another beautiful little girl. I called her Alicia Avril Winifred. She was perfect. This time, I was allowed home the very same day. It was unbelievable how different it all was. I was a mum again, but this time there was no David to come between us. For now.

My eighteenth birthday was a few weeks later and, to be honest, it was like any other day. For an exhausted mum of two, it seemed silly to go through the traditional celebrations of reaching adulthood. I had been forced to grow up far too quickly, so, in my head, I had reached that age many years earlier. Now I was just mesmerised by my new baby and determined that no one would ever hurt her the way David had hurt me.

But, despite my joy at my lovely little girls, there was a dark cloud on the horizon. Alicia was only a few months old when Mum called me up, breathlessly excited.

'We've had some wonderful news, pet!'

My mind whirled with the possibilities. Had they won some money? Had Dad got a new job?

'That's great Mum. About time you had a bit of good luck.'

'It's David.' Her voice was warm and happy, but my heart felt like it had iced over.

'Oh?' I managed to croak.

'Yeah, I just got the call. He's up for early release. He could be out any day now! Isn't that amazing? I'm so happy for him and Nicola. And he'll finally get to meet his new niece.'

'Yes. Great,' I said, trying to keep my voice steady. 'Look Mum, I've got to go. Alicia needs feeding.' But after I hung up the phone, I didn't move. I just stood like a statue, overcome with fear about the future. The nightmare was beginning again, but this time I had two little girls to protect.

Life might not have been easy since David had been inside, but I had definitely felt less anxious. Now my brother was due out any week and I knew my life was going to start an entirely new chapter. I'd changed a lot since David had been sentenced, and, facing him as an adult and a mother of two, I knew I was a stronger person. Still, I had no idea how I would cope when he reappeared in our lives.

12

Goodbye Dad

Initially I'd been terrified that David was going to come home and live with us when he got out of prison, as I was sure Mum would open her arms and welcome him home. I tried to discreetly find out what his plans were but with no luck. Then, the week he was being released, Mum and I were sitting together one morning having breakfast and feeding Kirsty when she sighed and said: 'Just so you know. David's decided not to come home. He's going to stay with his mate, Tim.'

I was so relieved. Inside I wanted to jump with joy but obviously I couldn't show any of it.

'Oh, OK,' I managed, and walked away, relief flooding over me. It was worth living behind a mask if it meant David stayed the hell away from me and my daughters.

Two weeks after his release, David still hadn't come to visit Mum and Dad. Mum was desperate to see him, and even though seeing him was the last thing on my mind, I felt for her. It was typical David: he didn't care about his parents waiting for him at home despite the way they'd stood by him every step of the way.

After the second week Mum was beside herself and so decided that, if he wouldn't come to us, she would go round to Tim's flat. I hoped she would go with Dad and leave me at home with Kirsty and Alicia, but she was insistent we went along too.

'Oh, Mum, he doesn't care about us,' I said. 'He'll probably just want to see you guys.'

But Mum wasn't having any of it.

'Don't be silly. He'll want to see you too,' she retorted. There was no way I could tell her that that's exactly what I was scared about.

The following day, Dad decided to drive, and while he and Mum were packing the car, I popped back to my bedroom and threw some LSD in my mouth. It was as flippant and irresponsible as that. A friend had bought the tabs round last week, but I'd been nervous of trying them. I can imagine what you must be thinking of me, but taking drugs was no big deal in the world I'd grown up in, and now I needed to get out of my head. I knew LSD would give me a completely different personality, numb my feelings, and prepare me for seeing David. The drug hit me almost instantly and, thankfully, my fear, and my sense of time and self completely changed. My insides felt like they'd flipped over and created a new person. I was so out of it I didn't speak for the entire journey.

When we arrived at Tim's flat, I stayed outside with Kirsty and Alicia and watched them playing on the grass. I didn't step one foot inside. I couldn't manage it. I heard Mum and Dad chatting with David about his plans and what life was like out of prison and it made my stomach churn. Even though the drugs had given me the extra strength to get in the car, hearing his voice still made my stomach flip. So I stayed away. After a while, Mum came out to find out what I was up to.

'Vicks, what are you doing? It's freezing out here!' she asked, arms folded across her chest.

'The girls are having fun,' I said, mind still swirling with the effects of the drugs, but I went completely cold as

David snaked through the door and looked right at me. He was completely expressionless, but his eyes bored right into me.

'Oh, David, Vicky's just in one of her funny moods,' Mum said brightly. 'But never mind. You were telling me about your plans.'

'Well, Nic knows some people who might set me up with a job,' he said, his eyes still roaming over me and my little girls. 'It's definitely time for a fresh start.'

My stomach was gripped with fear. I was literally frozen to the spot.

'What you lot doing out there?' my dad called from the kitchen. 'The kettle's boiled.'

Mum led David back inside. She couldn't stop touching him, as if she couldn't quite believe he was finally free, finally back with his family. Neither could I.

When it was time to leave, we all trooped out to the car. I kept my head down, trying to avoid David's eyes, but Mum called my name.

'Vicky, are you not going to say bye to your brother?'

My stomach muscles tensed up. 'Err, yeah, of course – see ya,' I said, with tears pricking my eyes. And, as the words left my mouth, my eyes locked with his for a few seconds. I could see the gloating in his eyes. He was hurting me again, and he was enjoying it.

'Bye, Vicky, look after yourself.' He made it sound like a threat.

I wrenched my eyes away, feeling dizzy with fear. David was free, and I was trapped.

I don't know what I would have done then if I hadn't spotted Tim. At one of the worst moments of my life he appeared just when I needed something to distract me from my misery. Tim had been David's friend since school and he'd often mentioned him, but we had never met before. Seeing him, I realised he was gorgeous and I couldn't drag my eyes away. With the LSD inside me, and adrenaline still coursing through my veins, Tim suddenly seemed like the answer to all my prayers. God knows I needed someone to protect me from David – and myself.

By eighteen, I was a heavy drug user. It was my only escape from the torturous thoughts in my mind. Although I didn't consciously say to myself 'I'm taking drugs because of what David did to me when I was twelve,' looking back it's obvious that that was my way of dealing with the hellish memories of the rapes.

As well as cannabis, I started taking speed and LSD whenever I could. I know it sounds awful, and many people would dismiss me as a druggie, but I never saw myself like that. Drugs were so freely available in my neighbourhood that it seemed almost inevitable that I would use them. With David free I would have tried anything to do away with the crippling fear of what he might do to keep me silent.

Over the next few weeks, David called Mum on a regular basis. At the end of the day, Mum still loved David and he still wanted her help with day-to-day problems. Once I picked up the phone and it was him.

'Hello?' There was silence. 'Hello,' I said again.

'Mum there?' he drawled. My stomach flipped. Just hearing his voice was enough to terrify me, so I just hung up and made a note to stop answering the phone.

But it wasn't only my brother who called.

'Vicky, Tim's on the phone for you,' Mum shouted one day.

I couldn't believe it. We chatted and flirted and soon it was a regular occurrence. He was a full-time lorry driver so whenever he passed he popped in to see me. Having a man take over my mind was the best possible distraction and so, with Tim occupying my thoughts, I found I could bury my fears about David – for a while, at least.

By summer 1992, Mum, Dad and the girls and I had moved to West Thurrock and I'd finally decided to get my own little flat. It was a tough call, but being around Mum and Dad so often – especially when I was a mum myself – made me feel like I'd never really grown up. Besides, my relationship with Tim was blossoming, and I was starting to dream of setting up as a proper little family.

'I'm going to apply for a council flat, Mum,' I mentioned nervously one day.

She didn't look up straight away, but when she answered she had a smile on her face.

'I knew this time would come eventually,' she said.

Dad came and gave me a hug. I was eighteen and, with the support of Tim and my parents, I finally felt ready to stand on my own two feet.

However, I knew there would be a huge decision to be made about Kirsty. Even though she was my daughter, Mum had basically brought her up. I was so young when I had her that it was only natural that Mum and Kirsty had bonded. There was only thirteen years age difference between me and Kirsty – more like sisters than mother and daughter. She even called her gran 'Mum', while I was 'Vicky-sister-mum'. At first it didn't hurt me – when I was struggling during the early years I was glad she had Mum – but now, it was difficult. Now I had Alicia I was a much more confident mother and I wanted Kirsty with me. My dream was to provide her and Alicia with a stable home – and, if everything went according to plan, a father figure who would love them like my dad had loved me. But was she really better off with a teenage mum who had another baby to care for? How could I take Kirsty from Mum when it'd hurt them both so much? And how could I protect my daughter, when I couldn't even protect myself? So when Mum asked to keep Kirsty with her, I didn't object.

'Of course, Mum,' I said. 'Kirsty is best with you, and anyway, I'm only down the road.'

Unfortunately, so was David.

Later that year, I finally moved into my very first home with Alicia and it seemed an amazing accomplishment. The flat was on Roseby Road, about two miles from Mum and Dad's. It was far enough to feel some kind of independence, but close enough to pop round for dinner or a cup of tea. One way or another, Mum, Dad and I still saw one another on a daily basis, and Tim popped round whenever he could. Kirsty even came to stay every other weekend and I'd make a big fuss of her when she was with me. As Alicia was so young, I'd put her to bed and Kirsty and I loved sitting on the sofa chatting. We'd end up giggling over the silliest things – daft stuff that the dogs had done or Mum burning the dinner because she was too busy talking. I loved hearing her chat away. Considering what we'd both been through and the situation we were in, we were very close.

One of the best parts about having my own flat was being able to see Tim in private. I started to really fall for him and I just loved being with him. It made me realise how lovely it'd be to have a family of my own – a flat, children and a man to love. It was all I ever wanted and I think I started to see Tim and me in a serious relationship far quicker than he did. I may have looked like an adult, but inside I was still a scared little girl, looking for a prince to save me.

*   *   *

One thing got in the way of my fairytale ending, though: my wicked brother. Sometimes Tim would talk about David – he was his friend after all – but I always quickly made him change the subject. 'Do we have to talk about my stupid criminal of a brother?' I'd joke, hoping he wouldn't see how deadly serious I was. Other times Tim would want David to come round. I protested as much as I could, saying the children would be in bed, and claiming that David was really loud, until eventually they arranged to meet elsewhere. It was difficult to lie to the man I loved, but the most important thing was that David was away from me and my girls.

Another problem Tim and I had was my issue with jealousy. It wasn't something that usually affected me but Tim was so good-looking that it made me very insecure, wondering whom else he fancied and who fancied him, because I didn't have a lot of confidence in myself. I'd always struggled with my weight, and after two kids I sometimes felt frumpy. How could I compete with a carefree teenager my own age, for example, who had nothing but shopping and celebrity gossip to worry about?

Apart from trying to keep my jealousy under control, though, the early days were fabulous. David lived with his wife at first but as soon as he had his release tag removed, he and his wife split. I never really got to the bottom of what happened there, but it was a lucky escape for Nicola. To be honest, I don't think David had it in him to genuinely care about another human being. David would travel around the south after that, seeing old friends, always out and about again, and so Tim was free to devote all his time to me. Tim used to pick me up in his lorry and we spent a lot of time together chatting, laughing and making love. It was the first time I'd ever felt so happy – I thought it was too good to be true. Tim was everything I'd been looking for in a man. He was friendly with everyone, cheeky, tall and handsome – the type of man all the women loved but all the men hated.

Alicia's dad, Mark, had been around quite often and had been doing a lot with Alicia since she was born. I was pleased we stayed friends and grateful that at least one of my girls had a solid father figure. But as soon as I got involved with Tim, Mark got very jealous and stopped coming round. Thankfully, he still kept up the contact with Alicia, but our friendship dwindled away. Tim and the girls became my everything for a while; nothing else mattered.

But then Dad fell ill.

Dad was never one to go to the doctors. He was simply never an ill person, and never even suffered with a cold. But, at the end of 1992, he started complaining of chest pains. When he went to the doctors they told him he had a chest infection and sent him away with antibiotics. When the pains didn't improve he went back, and this time he was sent to the hospital for an X-ray. Within a few days they had the results and they could see a dark patch on his lungs.

I knew it was bad even before Mum and Dad broke the news to me. A few members of our family had died of cancer so even though no one confirmed that's what Dad had, deep inside of me I already suspected it and I was panic-stricken. To me cancer equalled death and I couldn't imagine that nightmare happening. I tried my best to be strong for Dad, but inside a childish voice kept saying how unfair it was. After everything, surely I wasn't about to lose my beloved father too? I'd already had so much pain and misery in my life, missing out on so much fun and happiness – was it fair that I had to go through this too? It felt like pain was all I knew. Darkness filled my days, and it didn't look like it was going to change.

The following week Dad had one test after another. While I looked after the girls, Mum was with Dad every step of the way. One night, we'd just eaten dinner when she said to me: 'I think it's cancer, you know.'

I just looked at her, knowing she was right, but not wanting to believe or accept it. Dad had always been such a healthy person, how could he be so ill?

'He's a fighter, Mum,' I said. 'He'll be fine.'

I hoped with all my heart it was true.

'Don't say anything to your Dad' Mum warned. 'He's got enough on his plate just trying to get better.'

I suppose it was a surprise that Mum even talked to me about it because we weren't a talking family. We kept our feelings and emotions to ourselves. Even if we knew we were in a bad situation, we still wouldn't turn to one another – it just wasn't the way things were done in our family. Maybe it was one of the reasons why I never turned to anyone when David raped me? But now, when Dad was ill, we still didn't talk. There were nights Dad would be clenching his hands in pain, his face turning red with frustration. But still none of us could talk about it. I'd manage a 'You OK, Dad?' and he'd just nod his head and try to smile.

Mum and Dad continued to travel back and forth to the hospital and, by the third week of his illness, whatever Dad had on his lungs had doubled in size. It was the confirmation we needed that it definitely was cancer. He was still in his forties. I was heartbroken, utterly devastated and terrified. But being who I was I pretended to be very matter of fact about it all. Even though Mum was in pieces, I refused to be emotional about it.

'He'll be fine Mum – he won't leave us,' I said, holding Mum as she cried. For once, I was the strong one. My parents had done so much for me after Kirsty was born; I owed it to them to stay strong.

Once I'd learnt Dad really did have cancer, I made myself believe he'd fight it and be back to his old self in no time. Dad's doctor kept making more and more appointments for him to have scans and we had to just wait. Looking back, the whole process was painfully slow. We all know that speed is imperative with cancer, but it took ages for Dad to receive a final scan diagnosis. In fact, it was only a frightening turn for the worse that forced the doctors to tell us.

Just before Christmas, Dad went with Mum and Aunt Chris to get a tree from the local garden centre. 'Are you sure you'll be OK?' Mum asked Dad. Despite the pain he was in, he wanted to make Christmas really special for me and the girls.

'I'll be fine, Avril. We have to get a tree, and there's no way I'm letting you carry it on your own,' he said, smiling. So off they went while I stayed at home with the girls. I was clearing up the kitchen when I got the call.

'Mum, is that you?' I asked. I couldn't make out who it was through the sobs.

'We're at the hospital,' she said, her voice cracking. Dad had collapsed in pain at the garden centre and they needed to call an ambulance, which took them straight to Basildon Hospital.

'They want to keep him in,' Mum went on. 'I'm scared, Vicky.'

I didn't know what to say. I never knew what the right things were to say in emotional situations. But I knew Dad had a real battle on his hands. I put down the phone and ran out of the room, so that Alicia and Kirsty wouldn't see how upset I was.

Aunt Chris took Mum shopping that afternoon to get Dad some pyjamas, because he never wore bedclothes for bed and Mum wanted him to look his best, even in hospital. When Mum got back to the hospital a few hours later, Dad was hooked up to an oxygen mask and was very weak. She told me later that a consultant took her aside and explained how serious it was.

'You do realise that your husband is a very ill man?' he said. 'I'm more than sure it's cancer.' But Mum didn't want him to tell Dad, as she was sure he'd lose the will to fight if he knew.

'Can you let me tell him in my own time?' she asked. The consultant agreed.

When Mum told me we were sitting at the kitchen table. I was just playing with my fingers. I had no idea what to do or what to say.

'I think your father knows anyway,' Mum added. 'He's not stupid. I just don't know what I'd do without him.'

'Oh, Mum.' I took her hand across the kitchen table and we just sat there like that. The kettle boiled but neither of us could get up. I couldn't even cry.

Every day after that I'd gather my things to go and visit the hospital, and every day I'd end up breaking down at the thought of how ill my beloved father was. It didn't seem fair to burden him with my anguish when he needed all his strength to fight for his life. Also, in a strange way, I felt like treating him like a patient would be like admitting defeat. I just couldn't bring myself to see him in such a vulnerable state; it broke my heart too much. Rather than discuss his illness, I talked endlessly to the girls about the things we would do when Granddad was better, the fun we'd have when Granddad was home. So, in the end, I didn't go and see Dad in hospital. Instead, I committed myself to the practicalities of keeping things running smoothly at home. I found it too painful to think of him hooked up to monitors and other equipment while he lay weakly in bed. I'd been used to having my dad as my tower of strength, full of laughs. Seeing him in such a mess went against everything I knew of him, and I couldn't handle it. Since David had raped me, I'd become expert at shutting off parts of my mind – I'd had to be, otherwise the painful thoughts and feelings would have overpowered me. Now, in order to get up in the morning, I had to shut out the dreadful truth of what was happening to Dad.

One night, Mum said: 'Dad understands why you're not visiting him in hospital.'

I was so relieved, I cried. I don't cry often so many people thought I was cold, but this time I cried like I'd never stop. Dad knew I loved him and that I thought the world of him. Having him still understand me so well even when he was so ill made me even more emotional. It meant the world to me.

As the days and weeks passed Dad wasn't getting any better and, at night, when I was alone, thoughts of life without him pierced my brain. I sobbed and sobbed on my own. Tim didn't really know how to handle me when I was upset and I always tried to hide it from him. I much preferred to cry alone – it was what I was used to.

Dad was the only man in my life who had been consistently strong and reliable. I kept wondering what Mum and I were going to do without him. Mum and I had always had a patchy relationship but I suppose we really came together during Dad's illness. We had to be a team and I was grateful that Mum didn't pressure me into visiting Dad in hospital.

Thankfully, by the following week, Dad was a lot stronger and the hospital released him. When I saw him, tears pricked my eyes – he looked so thin and weak – but I refused to cry and make it worse for him.

'Oh, I've missed you, Vicky,' he said, giving me a hug. It was so hard keeping the tears back.

While he was home Mum took him to Southend Hospital to see another consultant for a second opinion and finally the consultant there took some action. He confirmed Dad had cancer, which we all knew already, and he immediately made the necessary appointment for him to have radiotherapy and chemotherapy, starting straight away. It was about time. Before that it had felt like none of the doctors cared enough to do anything. To them we were just another family from a council estate. Now Dad was finally getting the treatment he desperately needed. We could only hope that it wasn't too little, too late.

I felt so numb about my Dad's illness, like it was happening to another family. It just didn't seem real, so I took on the role of making sure everything was still running properly at home while Mum kept Dad going.

Over a period of weeks, Dad lost the use of his legs and he was very down. The consultants confirmed he would need a wheelchair and he'd never be able to drive again. He'd been in hospital for weeks having treatment and then he was allowed home for a while. A friend of the family got straight to the point.

'Are you sending Len home to die?' she asked the consultant, but they refused to commit to any answer.

'He'll enjoy his time at home with his family,' was all the doctor would say.

Just before Dad arrived home, Tim and I went over to Mum's to check she was OK and we walked in on her trying to move the bed from her bedroom to the dining room on her own. She was trying so hard to be strong. Tim and I quickly took over, but there seemed something horribly final about the bed being downstairs. We knew Dad would never make it upstairs again.

To make matters worse, David was around a lot because of Dad's illness. I suppose it meant he did have a heart somewhere inside of him but I don't know how much he really cared about it all. I couldn't imagine him having feelings for anyone except himself. It was hard having to see David so often, but, to tell you the truth, Dad was more important. I just kept myself busy with the girls and Dad, and it stopped me thinking about my brother.

Even while Dad was home I found it hard seeing him so ill. One day, I managed to perch my bum on the side of the bed and take his hand.

'You look well, love,' Dad croaked. But I couldn't meet his eyes. He was so thin and white, a shadow of his former self. I just held his hand so he knew I was there, but wasn't able to speak or look at him. I felt awful. He was my beloved father, but I couldn't face the reality of his illness.

Within days of his final homecoming, Dad fell really ill and suffered terrible sickness and diarrhoea. Mum called an ambulance and he was rushed back to hospital. It was very scary. It felt like we were just waiting for him to go. I was often very close to catching a taxi and visiting him at the hospital, but Mum would call instead and tell me how he was doing. I just couldn't bring myself to go. Seeing him so ill crushed me, so seeing him in a hospital ward would be even worse. I was only nineteen and I didn't want those images in my head for the rest of my life. Dad understood. He told Mum that I should be with my girls, and that he couldn't bear his little girl to see him looking like a corpse. Even wracked with pain my dad was still a proud, dignified man.

One night, Tim and I were sitting in the living room when David turned up out of the blue. My veins turned to ice.

'Hi, mate!' Tim called. 'What've you been up to?'

'Just got back from the hospital.' His voice was low and dangerous. 'Where have you been, Vicky, you selfish bitch?'

'Lay off her. She's been here with the kids,' Tim said, trying to calm him down.

'How is he?' I whispered. It took all my strength to speak.

'What do you care? I think it's disgusting that you haven't been to see Dad,' he started shouting. 'What kind of person are you? He's dying and you're sitting at home.'

David was the only person I'd ever been scared of, but I was angry too. How dare he accuse me of being a bad person! I moved to the kitchen but he followed me, taunting me.

'You're nothing. You're worse than nothing. Mum can't believe you're doing this.' At this I spun round.

'What do you care? You don't care about anyone!' I'd never talked back to him before, and he looked like he would explode with anger. I was about to speak again, but before the words had left my mouth his hands were around my throat.

In his temper, David had grabbed my neck and tightened his fingers around it. I was choking for breath, my arms flailing. Is this how Helen died? I thought, is this what it feels like? My brother pinned me to the bed I'd brought down for Dad and I couldn't move. I saw Tim jump on his back, trying to stop him, but it was no good. David was so strong and he wasn't going to let go of his grip on my neck. His fingers tightened and I couldn't even scream any more. I thought he was going to kill me. I genuinely believed the time had finally arrived – the moment I'd always feared would happen – and that he was going to finally destroy me. This proved everything I had ever been scared of: the moment I'd stood up to him, he strangled me. What would happen to my girls now? Who would look after them? I gasped for breath, but the air became thinner and my gasps became shorter. Next minute I blacked out. Everything vanished.

When I woke up, Tim was standing over me with a wet flannel, calling my name. I felt really light-headed and dizzy but as soon as my mind and eyes focused, everything flooded back to me like a bad nightmare.

'Where is he?' I screamed, standing up quickly. But as soon as I moved I felt sick, and I vomited over the floor. I was as white as a ghost and every time I moved I was ill.

'As soon as you collapsed that bastard bolted,' Tim said, stroking my hair. 'Where the hell did that come from?'

I ignored his question. Where would I begin?

'What about Kirsty and Alicia? Are they OK?'

'They're upstairs, love.'

'They didn't see anything?'

'No. At least we don't have to worry about that.'

'Thank God,' I said, hugging my knees.

'Christ, Vicky, I thought he'd killed you. I thought he'd really killed you.'

Tim's voice was unsteady.

'You went so blue. I've never been so scared in my life. I know he's your brother, but I'm going to kill that bastard.'

'No!' I tried to stand up. 'No. We'll keep away from him. We will have nothing to do with him. Do you promise?'

Reluctantly, Tim promised to do whatever I wanted. I had tried to stand up to David and it had almost killed me. There was no way I was risking him hurting anyone else I loved.

That night I tossed and turned in bed, not knowing what to do about David. Should I tell Mum what he was really like? She had so much on her plate already with Dad's illness, how could I put this burden on her too? In the end I decided not to tell her about David trying to strangle me. I was allowing him to get away with it again, but my hands were tied. I couldn't tell Mum about her son now. It felt like history was repeating itself, and it was at the worst time imaginable. Dad's condition was deteriorating and Mum was at the hospital all day, every day. She told me that one night Dad told her he couldn't go on. 'I can't fight any more, Avril,' he'd said. 'I don't think I'm going to make it this time.' When I heard this, I felt like I couldn't go on either.

Two weeks later, Dad died. The day is etched in my memory for life. I was with Tim in the lorry for the day and he'd just dropped off some goods at Spitalfields market in London. Suddenly, I got a feeling – something just came over me, like a cold shiver. I knew something was wrong.

'Tim, we need to go, something has happened to Dad,' I said.

'What do you mean?' he asked, bewildered.

'I don't know, but please hurry – I need to see Dad,' I screamed.

Tim drove as fast as he could from the centre of London to Basildon Hospital, in Thurrock. He trusted my instincts so much he was spinning round corners.

Tim dropped me off outside the hospital and I bolted up the stairs and into Dad's room. I opened the door and everyone was still and quiet. Silent sobs filled the room. He had died ten minutes before I got there.

'He's gone, love,' Mum cried. I was completely out of breath from running. My heart felt like it had collapsed.

'I knew it, I knew it,' I started to sob. I'd just known deep down inside that he was going to leave me. I was devastated to have missed him, and I cried like a little girl. I spotted David standing in the corner of the room staring, but I was so overwhelmed with grief and sadness that for once I didn't even care that he was there. My Dad, the man I'd looked up to for so long, the only person who had ever truly loved me, was gone.

Mum was in pieces. She sobbed and sobbed but I couldn't help her; I was a mess myself. As I lay on my knees holding Dad's cold hand, all kinds of thoughts ran through my mind. The thought of living the rest of my life without him seemed impossible. Dad had always been there for me, and even though he hadn't been able to protect me from David, it helped during the aftermath to have him there to love me. Now he was gone, never knowing what David did to me. And I was glad. If Dad had known, it would've shattered him into little pieces.

I said goodbye to my precious father one last time, but, as I got up, I caught David's eye. It suddenly dawned on me that he would relish the thought that I was even more vulnerable now. Dad wasn't around for me any more, and Mum had always been blind to her son's dark side. David had already got away with raping me and throttling me, and I was terror-stricken about what else he was capable of.

The days after Dad's death were bleak, dark and miserable. Life seemed pointless now he was gone. We tried to get on with everyday chores and responsibilities, but it seemed so pointless. Dad's sister, Aunt Chris, was wonderful and helped us all, but it was hard to get motivated.

'What are we going to do without him, eh?' I'd say to little Alicia.

When I saw Kirsty she would hug me tightly. It was heartbreaking for her too. Dad thought the world of Kirsty, and she had lost the only father figure in her life.

'He'll be watching us,' I tried to comfort her. 'He won't ever leave us. I'm sure he's with us now.' Even to my ears, though, the words sounded dull and empty.

We cremated Dad on Christmas Eve. I got up that morning and took a shower feeling numb. I pulled on the black suit that Dad had bought me and as soon as I was ready I pulled out my little box of tobacco and rolling papers and got stoned. It was completely irresponsible, but at that stage I couldn't cope with anything emotional or difficult without drugs. My father was dead, my brother had tried to kill me and my silence was weighing heavier on my heart than ever.

Later that morning Dad's hearse arrived, followed by a car to take us to the crematorium. I chose not to see Dad again. Mum had been to say her last goodbyes at the chapel of rest, but I couldn't. It was like the hospital all over again: I wanted to think of Dad taking me fishing, or holding court behind the bar, not laid out on a cold slab. The rest of that day went by in a blur. David hovered like a bad smell, acting like the doting son, holding and helping Mum along the way. He even managed to slip in front of me and sit next to Mum in the pew. But I can honestly say that, compared to the heartbreaking emotions I was feeling, David was a distant thought. I didn't even cry that day. I felt it inside but the tears stayed locked away. Mum was inconsolable; it was heartbreaking in itself just watching her. She adored my father and I know she was finding it hard to think of the future without him. I shivered when I thought of it. We seemed so lost and vulnerable.

After the funeral we had a few people back to the house for a drink and some food, but I wasn't in the mood to mix. I crept upstairs and smoked all afternoon. I didn't even want to see Tim. Even though I had two daughters to care for, on that day I was a child again, a teenage girl who had just lost her daddy. The more I smoked the more numb I felt, while David acted like the responsible man of the family downstairs. Maybe I should have joined him and made people see I was the strong one in our family? But I couldn't. That day I just didn't have the strength to pretend everything was OK.

Mum never came up to see me or check on me. She knew I was struggling but she left me to deal with my emotions alone, which was what I was used to. Instead, she and David put on a united front: grieving mother and model son. If only our friends and family had seen the ugliness beneath his caring mask.

The following day was Christmas and it was the worst Christmas day ever. Mum normally cooked an amazing dinner, but not that year. Aunt Chris kindly invited us round and fed us instead. Opening presents and pulling crackers just didn't seem the same. What was there to celebrate? But it was Dad's favourite time of year, so I knew that I had to make an effort for his sake. I knew he could never imagine not celebrating Christmas.

'Cheer up!' Kirsty kept on saying, trying to help. She and Alicia were just children, and, despite their loss, all they wanted to do was open presents and have fun. But it was the last thing I wanted to do.

'What's in your cracker then?' I tried. But acting happy and jolly when we were feeling so raw inside was horrendous.

David had gone to see his current girlfriend so thankfully he was out of the picture, but the day passed by in a cloud of grief.

Life was hard with Dad gone. Mum just couldn't pick herself up and I felt like I was the backbone of our family, looking after the girls and making sure our homes were running smoothly. David vanished and went to stay with friends. Meanwhile, I really started to feel the pressure. Days merged into weeks and Kirsty came to live with me. As soon as the girls were ready in the morning I went round to see Mum, but she would be a mess. She was always crying, still in her pyjamas, and refusing all offers of food.

'Mum, please eat,' I'd beg. 'Dad wouldn't want to see you like this.'

But she never answered. She had no motivation for anything and I could see her falling apart in front of my eyes.

For a while, Mum's sister came to stay and help out. It was a huge relief. But one day in February I got a call from her.

'Your Mum isn't getting any better. I think I need to take her to hospital,' she said.

It was a huge shock. I knew Mum was finding it hard to move on but I didn't suspect she was having a breakdown.

'Tim will take you' I said, as I had to stay home with the girls. Tim came home later that day and said the doctor had decided to keep Mum in. In the end, I decided it was for the best too. It was obvious she needed some help and I felt powerless to do anything for her. Mum and I hadn't always been close, but seeing her turn from a strong, confident woman into a quivering wreck tore my heart out. When she most needed him, however, her darling boy was nowhere to be seen.

A few weeks later Mum was admitted to Gray's Mental Hospital with depression. She was crying continuously, with no enthusiasm for life. It was heartbreaking, really. I managed to visit her a couple of times, but she didn't even know I was there.

'Hi Mum,' I would say clearly. 'Kirsty and Alicia say hi.'

But she was drowsy after her medication and could barely talk. Walking back from the hospital, I'd try not to think about how alone I felt. Everyone was relying on me to hold it together.

Just when I thought things couldn't get any worse, my beautiful dog Ben went missing. He was about ten years old by then and one night he was just gone. Tim, the girls and I looked for him everywhere, calling his name up and down the streets. I was worried sick. I'd heard that dogs leave home when they're going to die, that they know when the time is coming and quietly slip away to a peaceful corner. That would have been typical of my gorgeous, loving dog, but the last thing I needed was to lose Ben too. It seemed everything strong and supportive in my life was fading away. I know dogs don't live for ever, but I never allowed myself to accept that Ben would one day leave me. After a few days of waiting and searching, it was obvious that he'd either been run over or had slunk away to die. I was gutted, but I still didn't cry. I found that, the older I was getting, the less able I was to let the tears fall. In the end, we never found his body.

While Mum was getting help, I decided to leave my flat and move back home. It was around this time I also started feeling unwell myself but I didn't give it too much thought. The girls were living on dry cream crackers and baked beans for weeks because we had no money, so being a bit off-colour was the least of my worries. I'd always struggled for money, but we now had even less without Mum helping. Plus, I found out many years later that when David visited Mum in hospital he took her bankbooks and she gave him money, telling him he had to share it with me, but he never did. Apparently he lived on daily take-aways and had trips out, all while the girls and I struggled to feed ourselves properly.

I carried on for weeks while still feeling rough and then the obvious dawned on me – I was pregnant! I did a home pregnancy test and it was positive. It was a huge shock. I'd been taking the pill religiously since having Alicia because I just couldn't afford another baby, but something had obviously gone wrong. Yet, in another way it was the nicest news possible. As one life ended, another began, and in some way it made sense to me.

When I told Tim he was over the moon, and, as word got around the family, it proved to be the happy news we all needed to pick us up after a terrible past few months. But living in the house where Dad had been ill was hard, so, after Mum was released from hospital in April, Tim and I decided we all needed a fresh start in Littleport, Cambridgeshire. Tim sorted out a caravan for us until we found a house and Mum came with us. After a hard and sad winter, it was a lovely summer, and I remember living in cut-off dungaree shorts while Alicia and Kirsty skipped about in cute little embroidered gypsy tops.

I think Tim was the first boyfriend I ever truly loved, but increasingly I worried that he didn't love me. After a while, I could see he was getting fed up. He spent more and more time away from home, and consequently I became very jealous and paranoid.

'Where have you been?' I asked one night when he got back after the kids were in bed.

'Work was busy,' he said, hanging up his jacket and not meeting my eye.

'So why didn't you call and let me know?' I asked, trying to keep my voice light.

'God, Vicky, what is it? Am I being interrogated?' And he'd walk off, never wanting to talk.

He started to lose patience with me and so we'd argue, which made him stay away even more. It was a vicious circle. He even stopped giving me money for food shopping and new shoes for the girls and gave me the brush-off whenever I tried to be affectionate. But I never wanted to admit to myself that we had serious problems. I suppose I'd been kidding myself for a long time, thinking I had a perfect little family, and a man who loved me and was going to stand by me. Also, I was pregnant, so I needed him and I didn't want to face another birth on my own. I was tired of being alone; I wanted someone to care for me. I felt I did everything I could to try and make him happy, but it was never enough.

After giving birth to little Samantha Jane in August 1993, I was elated – she was just beautiful. Tim was happy too, acting like the proud father, especially as she looked so much like him. But soon the happy baby bubble burst and Tim and I began to argue even more. He went off for days and I wouldn't hear from him. As he was a lorry driver, he had a very good excuse, but before I used to get regular calls from him or he'd come home for his lunch. I also started having the contraceptive injection a few months after giving birth to Sam. The doctors had done lots of tests and they concluded the pill just wasn't right for me, but, with the injection, my problems went from bad to worse. Within three months of taking it my weight was out of control and, eventually, I ballooned from a curvy size 12 to a size 26, and my weight issues only put extra stress on my relationship with Tim. My insecurities just kept growing because I felt so ugly. I began to accuse him of everything. The jealousy I'd built up inside just exploded and I was devastated that all my fears about him were coming true.

Sam was only a few months old when her father went missing for several days together. I was worried sick, imagining he'd been hurt. When he came home with no explanation, I finally lost it.

'Do you not love us? What's wrong with us?'

He wouldn't even look at me, and by the end I was screaming with rage.

'I can't take this Vicky,' he said. 'You're unbearable.'

I watched in a daze as he threw his things into his truck and slammed the door behind him. There wasn't even a goodbye. I listened to my children moving in their beds upstairs and a deep sense of hopelessness filled my insides. When was the misery and abandonment going to end?

For years I'd been looking for my knight in shining armour, someone who I could completely lean on to look after me. I thought I'd found him in Tim and I wanted us to work. Having him let me down was just another reason to think all men were rotten apples; just more proof that

I wasn't worthy of love and happiness. It made me think about my dad a lot and I wondered if I was going to ever find as good a man as he had been. Had David broken me so badly and my spirit so completely that I couldn't even recognise a good man if I found one?

Over the next few years, Tim was in and out of my life like a yo-yo. I suppose I was hoping he'd take me back so I stupidly let myself be at his beck and call. I was acting pathetically, really, but I was so desperate to be loved and cared for that I still hoped he'd see the light and come back to us. Perhaps he was using me. I gave him sex whenever he wanted it. I was craving some tenderness and a father for Sam, but one day he asked me if I'd have sex with his friend. I was utterly shocked that the man I loved and trusted could suggest such a thing. It was like someone finally switched on a light in my head. I closed the door on him and never saw him again. Me and the girls were worth more than that.

Tim didn't try to contact Sam or me again. He just vanished. I felt so sad for Sam. Another of my girls was fatherless. I had no idea how to break out of the cycle of neediness and rejection I was stuck in. What was I doing wrong? My girls needed a dad and I felt like I was failing them.

After Tim and I split for the last time, I stopped the contraceptive injections. No doctor had confirmed that the injections and my weight gain were connected, but, as soon as I stopped having them, the weight fell off. It was a relief to look like myself again, but, as a busy mum of three, I still had little time to worry about hair and clothes like the other twenty-year-olds I saw. I couldn't imagine what it would be like to be so carefree.

In the meantime, I'd started to get friendly with a local man called Tom. I met him through a neighbour and, admittedly, I got too close with him too quickly after Tim left because I was on the rebound. I was so fragile and hurt after Tim that Tom's arrival in my life felt like perfect timing.

With Tom, everything was very different. We had an understanding with one another that I'd never had with a man before. We had our own lives, families and homes and we'd come together when we wanted some company. After what I'd been through with Tim, having my feelings pulled through a mixer, I was actually OK with just being in a casual relationship. I think I can safely say we never loved one another, but we definitely grew to care for each other. But, stupidly, I fell pregnant again. I have to say that this time I wasn't careful, because I had started to realise I wanted a big family. While men kept walking all over me and coming in and out of my life, I knew that my children would never leave me. I have grown up a lot since then and know now that it was a damaging way to behave, but back then I just loved the fact that I had my little pack of family. It felt like having children and running a family was the only thing I could control and do well. Finding a man to love me wasn't happening, but I could have a big family around me, and love and be loved. The more children I had, the more I loved them and the more I wanted. Nine months later, I had Jamie Leonard Alan, my first son, and he was adorable. Father or no father, I swore that my children would enjoy the sort of happy, innocent childhood I'd had torn away from me.

I was now in my early twenties and wherever I went, Mum wasn't far behind; we stuck together and we always moved in unison. David, on the other hand, had been out of the picture for a while. It was obvious he didn't need anything, which explained why he wasn't pestering Mum so much.

Mum and I moved back to Tilbury in 1999. We reignited old friendships and it was lovely being close to Dad's sister, Aunt Chris, and my cousin Kate again. Life was tough living on a rough estate with four kids, though, and even harder when I found out I was pregnant again. My youngest son – little Kirk Philip, was born in April 2001. Unsurprisingly, Kirk's Dad didn't want to know, but I was used to that by now. Kirk was gorgeous, and I was determined to give my boy the best start I could.

It bothered me on a daily basis that my children didn't have a father figure in their lives, and I worried about what kind of an effect it was having on them. I had had a wonderful father, a person who showed me the way in life, but my kids didn't have that. As their mum, they were my number-one priority and I was never going to let them down, but I felt responsible for not being able to provide another parent for them. All I'd ever known in my adult life were unreliable men and, by now, I'd lost all hope of ever finding Mr Right. It was almost like I was deliberately choosing men who would abandon me, as if deep down I didn't think I was worthy of love. It was a cruel irony that the only father figure who was still in the picture was their Uncle David – the one man I hated and feared more than the devil himself.

13

A Wonderful Wedding

My little family and I moved back to Purfleet when I had Kirk, away from the noisy neighbours and the rough estate. After being back just a few months, a friend of mine announced her engagement and I was invited to her party. It was perfect timing because after a hellish few months I definitely needed a good time with friends. I was in my late twenties by then, with five kids, and I had lost my father, my mother was extremely fragile and my brother was a violent criminal who had already tried to silence me for good.

Looking back, I had a lot to cope with.

The party turned out to be a great night and, during the evening, I caught the eye of a guy I'd never met before. He was full of smiles and kept looking over. Eventually he introduced himself.

'Hi, I'm Kelly. I think I've seen you around town.'

He had a lovely voice, really warm and genuine. I was flattered that he'd noticed me, but I'd been burned too many times to lose my head over him – that night, at least!

The following night I invited a few friends over to my place to gossip about last night's party, and Kelly joined us. We ended up chatting all night. He made me laugh so much, and we bonded very quickly. Kelly was only a few years older than me and he told me he didn't really have any family left. I felt for him – I knew what it was like to lose someone you loved – but I also loved his wry sense of humour.

Kelly wasn't exactly gorgeous, but then, after Tim, I'd had enough of fickle, good-looking men to last me a lifetime. It's normally something about a guy's personality I go for, and Kelly seemed like a genuinely nice person. He kept hanging his arm over his armchair, so we'd brush against each other's fingers every now and then. There was a lot of chemistry between us and it was obvious he liked me; I liked him too. Kelly later told me that whenever he saw me at the school gates I intrigued him because I wasn't like the other mothers; I seemed more 'down to earth'. Likewise, he seemed more real than anybody I'd ever met.

That night we got on so well that Kelly never left. I know it sounds crazy but he just decided to move in. There was no official chat and I didn't even ask him – he just announced it. I made it clear that my children and I came as a package, but he was genuinely enthusiastic about joining my family. I thought his spontaneity was quite exciting, and he was completely honest when he told me he was in the middle of a split with an ex-girlfriend.

'Meeting you has made me realise that it should end,' he added. 'I want to be with you and your kids for ever.' I felt bad for his ex, but it was just what I wanted to hear. So, step-by-step, he moved his things over to mine. It's weird how it just happened so quickly. You'd think I'd be more cautious of sudden relationships as I got older, be a little bit more wary, but deep down I was still hoping that every man who gave me some attention would be the one who would love and protect me and mine for ever. Kelly seemed like a man who could shelter us from harm.

He certainly didn't shy away from commitment. Three days after we'd met, we were chatting in bed when Kelly just popped the question. Actually, it wasn't so much of a question as a statement – 'I want to spend the rest of my life with you. We should get married,' he said, serious as anything. It was crazy and it had all happened so fast, but I said 'yes', completely caught up in the moment. There was just something about him that made me feel safe. And, in hindsight, I suppose the previous few years had been so difficult that I felt I didn't have anything to lose. It was one of the best decisions I've ever made.

The next few months were amazing. Kelly and I had a lot of fun together and he was great with the kids. Kirsty was in her teens when I met Kelly and was still living at her gran's. My eldest had grown into a wonderful young lady; I was so proud of her. Considering where we lived and the type of people we called neighbours, she didn't mix with any bad crowds and had a very secure unit of friends around her. She'd turned out brilliantly. But, as Kelly got to know my family, he assumed Kirsty was my sister. He never asked me directly, but we were so close in age he never thought I might be her mother. To be honest, it was what a lot of people assumed. It was very confusing for other people, but it worked OK for us. Kirsty knew I was her biological mum, of course, but had never asked any questions. It was all she knew and she just accepted it in that wonderful way that kids do. And, as long as she was happy, that's all I cared about. I suppose I'd carried on living my life in a bubble, hoping the subject of her father would never come up. She was such a happy, polite and loving girl that I was sure she was content. Our family's situation was always going to be a tricky subject for people to understand so we were pretty private about it, until direct questions were asked. I was sure Kelly would find out one day if he stayed around long enough, so I never corrected him. I suppose part of me felt that, if Kelly didn't know I'd been pregnant at twelve, it would make the whole ordeal less real. David's attacks were old wounds but they were still deep, ugly ones, and I didn't want to show them to my fiancé just yet.

Kelly was very romantic. He regularly wrote me poems and left them around the house for me to find, or he'd text romantic messages. I wrote them all down so I'd never forget them: 'Good morning my love, just to let you know I love you'; 'I want to hold you so much. I love you so much.' I'd never been treated this way before and I found it hard to get used to.

'Have you got nothing better to do than text me all day?' I joked.

I just wasn't used to such a loving boyfriend and I didn't know how to respond. Whenever he gave me a compliment I shrugged it off – having nice things said to me was so alien. I had no self-confidence and I hated everything about myself, having been put down and treated so badly by men over the years. Kelly had a lot of work ahead of him if he wanted the same level of romance back.

Kelly was brilliant in lots of ways, but his real fault was that he regularly took speed. As I've said before, everyone in my life seemed to be taking drugs so when I found out Kelly did too I tried to brush it aside, concentrating on the fact he was a nice guy instead. But, after a few weeks, I realised it was going to cause a lot of problems for us. Taking speed meant Kelly never slept: he grabbed five-minute naps when he could but he never actually came to bed to sleep. So, in the end, I ended up joining him a couple of times after the kids were in bed. I found myself feeling completely out of control and, even though it was a great way to do the housework, it wasn't right for me. Kelly, though, was addicted, and it was harder for him to just give it up.

Kelly may have been addicted to speed, but his love and affection seemed to unleash something even darker in me. If he came back late from work I'd fly into a jealous rage, shouting and screaming and even getting violent. During one argument I grabbed Kelly's walking stick and slammed it over his back in my temper. There was so much force behind my blow that the stick split in two and it left a mark on Kelly's back. He looked at me and I could see the hurt in his eyes. Afterwards I felt so guilty I cried myself to sleep.

'What's wrong, Vicks?' Kelly asked. 'Why are you acting like this?'

'I'm sorry. I'm so, so sorry,' I'd whimper. 'I swear to you it'll never happen again.'

But I couldn't tell him what was really behind my terrifying fit of anger. I hated what I was doing but I just couldn't stop myself. It was like I was no better than David. I had hated my life for so many years, and I had locked up so many emotions for so long, that I was torn about by bitterness and it all came out at Kelly. I couldn't hurt David so instead I raged against the man I loved.

No matter what I did to Kelly, though, he always came home. I couldn't believe he hadn't walked away like so many before him. I think he proved to me that, no matter what we went through, he must love me, because he was sticking around.

In October 2002, we got married. I managed to find £400 for my wedding dress and Mum came with me to buy it.

Always being so busy I only allocated myself one day to find one so we went to this wedding shop and I tried loads on, but it wasn't until I tried the last one that I fell in love. The dress was gorgeous and fitted my figure perfectly, but I was so fussy I still wanted to change it. It had roses all around the neckline and although I liked them I thought there were too many.

'It's a shame there are so many roses, eh, Mum?' I moaned.

And Mum just gave me a smile. 'Don't worry, I can take a few off for you,' she reassured me. She was quite clever with a sewing machine and thread.

We weren't going to have a big party because we couldn't afford it but where we could, we splashed out. As Kelly was a great cook, he was in charge of the cake and he made three tiers: one was fruit, one was sponge and one was chocolate and heart shaped. All my girls were my bridesmaids and they had beautiful blue and lilac trouser-suits that mum had made and gorgeous baskets of flowers. After my Dad's death my relationship with my Mum had really deepened. She'd always been great on a practical level, but having nursed her through her grief and depression we were much more emotionally close now. I'd seen her at her most vulnerable, and now I was very protective of her. I only wished there was a way I could stop her doting on David without smashing apart all of our lives.

The night before the wedding the girls wanted to see me in my dress and I was happy to oblige. The atmosphere in the flat was very loving and excited. But, as I tried to pull the zip up, it broke. My heart almost fell to the ground. I just looked at Mum in despair.

'Don't worry, love,' she said, in her straightforward way. 'I'll sort it.'

Early the next morning she got up, bought a new zip and was sewing hours before my wedding. It was a bit stressful, but I was so grateful to Mum for saving the day.

We got married at Gray's register office. It was a beautiful day, but something was missing – my dad. I could feel his absence and amidst my happiness I couldn't help but be sad that he wasn't there to give me away. But when Kelly and I were told we were husband and wife I was so happy that I had tears in my eyes. I'd finally found my soul mate. I never thought it was going to happen and I still had to pinch myself on the day.

Our party was nothing glamorous – just a nice, simple gathering with friends and family. Kelly wrote a speech and another poem. It was beautiful. I felt very special.

Mid-evening we ran out of alcohol and food. We just hadn't expected the day to go on for so long. Turned out it was a party everyone wanted to be involved in. In the end I had to go to the supermarket, but I didn't want to take my wedding dress off. It was the most beautiful item of clothing I had ever owned and I wanted to keep it on for ever.

'I don't mind going,' a friend offered.

But I couldn't let a guest buy food and drink for my wedding reception. So I decided to go in my dress.

'It'll be fun,' I giggled.

So I caught the bus to the supermarket that was just down the road and everyone stared.

'I've just got married,' I smiled.

I loved saying the words. I don't think I'd ever been so happy. In the supermarket I was running up and down the aisles trying to be as fast as possible so I didn't miss much of the party. I must've looked a right sight.

It was a wonderful day and, most importantly, David wasn't invited. He'd gone up to Scotland and done one of his vanishing acts. Mum hadn't heard from him for ages. He was most probably with a new girlfriend and didn't want Mum for anything, so he stayed away. Despite Mum's quibbles, none of us made the effort to get in touch with him so it made the day so much happier. I thought that perhaps we were free of him for ever. I was wrong.

14

Poison

In fairytales, the wicked character always arrives at the happiest moment, but at least David had the grace to give us a few months of married bliss before coming back and casting his evil spell. But, all too soon my brother reappeared and started spending a lot of time at Mum's place. Although he was in his thirties, he had no money and no home and so he became completely dependent on Mum. Within no time at all, my life went from a dream to a nightmare. I'd thought my children and I were safe, but now David was back I had been thrown back into hell.

With Kelly around, me and my younger kids had some protection. But what about Kirsty? She was David's daughter, and had grown up into a beautiful young woman. How could I know that her father wouldn't hurt her, or try and turn her against me?

'Come and live with me, pet,' I begged. 'It's about time, isn't it?'

'What are you on about?' she laughed. 'That's the last thing you want when you've just got married. Anyway, Mum likes having me here, and there's more space.'

I opened my mouth to try to explain that she was in danger, but shut it again. Kirsty was so bright, confident and happy – so unlike me at her age that it seemed unthinkable to let her know the truth. How could she stand to hear that her strange uncle was really her father, and that she was the product of incestuous rape? She didn't deserve that. Instead, I spent day and night wracking my brains for a way to keep her safe from David.

As the weeks passed, my nerves were wearing thin, but, as I leant more and more on Kelly, he continued being the party animal he'd always been. I couldn't complain; it was one of the things I loved about him when we first met. He was happy and fun. But now David was back in our lives, I didn't have time for partying and good times.

At this point Kelly was taking so many drugs he was like a non-human, living on no sleep or food – utterly unbearable to live with.

'Kelly, I can't cope,' I screamed once, worn out by trying to pretend everything was OK.

'Oh, babe,' he'd whisper, hugging me. 'You know I love you.'

But my head was on the verge of exploding and I needed more than sugared words. One night I reached breaking point.

'Kelly, I love you, but I can't cope with the drugs any more – you have to pack them in,' I demanded. 'It's us or the drugs.'

He looked devastated that I had given him an ultimatum.

'I could never lose you and the kids,' he said slowly.

I cried with relief. I loved Kelly so much, and I needed his support to protect my family from David.

Soon Kelly was cutting the amount of drugs he was consuming a week in half, and within a few months he'd packed them in completely. His mind became a lot clearer and we began to act like a normal family. Well, almost.

Kelly must have wondered what was up because I started sending him on all sorts of strange errands.

'Can you call Mum and see if she's on her own tonight? I'll make her dinner if she is,' I'd ask him, or 'Why don't you drop Kirsty's maths homework back to her, and see what's going on at Mum's?' It was my way of finding out if David was around. My fear had grown into a phobia over the years, and I couldn't risk being in the same room as my brother. But at the same time I needed to know that he wasn't having anything to do with Kirsty, so I'd send Kelly round to Mum's on the flimsiest of excuses. To my relief, I discovered that David was staying with friends for the first few months. My gorgeous girl was safe and I'd bought myself some time to figure out what to do. When Kelly found out David had been in prison for killing Helen, he agreed that we shouldn't have anything to do with him. I felt weak with relief that someone else had realised how dangerous he was.

Kelly eventually met David when he unexpectedly came to visit us with Mum. I almost fainted when he walked into the room.

'Hiya, Vicky, we've just popped over to say hello,' Mum shouted as she came in. I hoped she meant she'd brought Kirsty with her, but then I saw him and my heart stopped. David lurked in the hallway, smiling strangely and glancing around at my home, at my children. I couldn't look at him. I'd been sitting on the sofa, but I jumped up and I couldn't keep still.

'Aren't you going to offer your big brother a drink? He's had a long day,' Mum asked.

'Upstairs you go, kids,' I said, a little too loudly. 'Give us some room down here.'

Kelly kept looking at me, questioningly.

'What's wrong?' he mouthed. But I couldn't answer him. How could I? He already knew David and I hated one another. I think he assumed it was normal sibling rivalry, but I could tell he was getting more suspicious.

Kelly peered round the corner and saw David standing in the hall while Mum chatted to Alicia and Sam on the stairs. They eyeballed each other but didn't speak. Kelly looked at me and pulled a face.

'He's so arrogant,' he whispered.

I could tell that everyone felt uncomfortable because no one was talking, except Mum. At the earliest opportunity, I shooed my girls away. They were annoyed, but there's no way I could stand them breathing the same air as their uncle. After just a few minutes Mum and David left, and I collapsed on the sofa in relief.

That night Kelly told me how surprised he was that Mum thought so much of David.

'It's obvious your Mum thinks of David as her blue-eyed boy,' he said.

'So you've noticed,' I replied, but stopped myself going further. I was glad that Kelly could see it too as it made me realise that I wasn't just imagining it. But it also strengthened my reasons for not telling Mum what David had done to me, even now. If Kelly could see how much Mum thought of David, without me having to say a word, how could I know she'd even believe me? I felt like only I had the power to break the spell that David had cast over our family, but that, by doing so, I'd destroy my mother and darling daughter's peace of mind for ever, and risk losing the precious family I still had left after Dad's death. But Mum had told me that David was moving back in with her full-time. How could I risk him hurting my girls the way he'd hurt me?

David staying at Mum's and constantly being so close again was driving me towards a nervous breakdown. I felt so trapped. My girls loved spending time at their Gran's, but that meant they were making themselves vulnerable. Kirsty was living with her father, without any idea of how dangerous he was. But it wasn't just her. Alicia loved her Gran so she spent a lot of time in her house, and Sam adored Kirsty so she was often there too. Over and over I reminded them of David's conviction for manslaughter and told them to stay away from him, but I was terrified that it wouldn't be enough. I'd rather die than see my girls suffer as I'd suffered, so I desperately tried to think of a way to keep them safe.

I tried to stop them going altogether, but I couldn't find the words to tell Mum and Kelly why I didn't want my girls within a foot of David. David had already tried to silence me once and I was scared to death about the consequences of standing up to him again. What if he took his rage out on one of my girls this time? I'd kept my secret for almost twenty years – a lifetime – and the thought of saying the words seemed literally impossible. I felt utterly trapped, hating myself for not being able to speak out, but feeling utterly powerless to protect my beloved daughters.

'We'll be fine, Mum. We're only going up to Gran's,' Alicia would say.

In her eyes, what on earth could go wrong at her grandmother's house? But, in my eyes, Gran's house was more dangerous than the streets – how could I explain that to them?

No matter how many times my daughters assured me I was being silly – of course they didn't talk to weird Uncle David – I was wracked with nightmares. Alicia was the same age as I'd been when David had raped me; it made my skin crawl having him so close to her. And Kirsty was almost eighteen so I was fearful of the way he would see her and what he'd do about it. Every day that passed with David still around seemed to increase the danger, and every day I kept my silence made it even more impossible to break it and banish David from my family for ever.

I took out all my stress and emotional turmoil on Kelly, who was convinced he was doing something to upset me. He'd ask: 'What's wrong? What have I done?' And I couldn't give him an answer. He thought I didn't love him, but it was the complete opposite – I loved him so much that he was the nearest thing I had to take out my frustrations on. My patience with people disappeared almost completely thanks to the secret torment I was going through. During one argument with Kelly I threw a computer printer out the window. I felt like I wanted to explode but didn't know how to relieve the tension other than by lashing out.

Kelly began to ask more questions.

'Why are you so irrational? You're losing it,' he said, bluntly.

'I know. I'm so sorry,' I'd say. 'I'll try not to take it out on you.'

Other times he'd ask: 'One minute you're happy, the next you're out of control. Who is doing this to you?'

I think he started to suspect something bad had happened to me to make me so temperamental. In a way I was desperate for him to ask me directly, to draw it out of me. It was how I felt with Mum after David raped me the first time. Sometimes I'd think: just ask me, go on, ask me! But he never did. After every terrible argument or fight, I cried with the guilt of what I was doing to Kelly and he began to see I didn't want to be this way, that I just had no control. I knew Kelly wasn't stupid, though. It was obvious I wasn't normal. When we were alone in bed at night he'd whisper: 'What's wrong, babe. Why are you like this? I know something is wrong.' But even when I opened my mouth, nothing would come out. I think I'd buried the words so deeply that they couldn't resurface. So I'd roll over and dismiss him.

'I'm tired, babe,' I'd lie, and then I'd spend the night thinking about how to keep my girls away from David.

Despite the appalling way I treated him, Kelly was a great ally and I often sent him over to Mum's to check on the girls and secretly see if my brother was there.

'If David is there bring the girls back with you – I don't want them talking to him, he's a bad influence,' I'd insist.

And Kelly used to come back and bad-mouth David. 'He never speaks, he just sits on that computer,' he moaned.

David was never polite and Kelly could sense his arrogance. But David had always shut himself off from most people. He was very self-absorbed and seemed to be entirely lacking in empathy for others. Whatever the reason for his behaviour, the effect was chilling.

David was like a dark cloud, capable of blocking out the brightest sun. Once we went to Bell Wood Park, near Ockenden, for the afternoon with a picnic. Mum and Kirsty came and we planned a lovely afternoon in the sunshine. We'd just arrived when David called Mum and said he was coming too.

'How nice! Your uncle is going to join us,' Mum said to the girls, and my skin went cold.

I saw Kelly looking at me but I carried on unpacking the car. Within a few minutes, Mum and I were sitting on a bench while the kids were playing near the water. But the afternoon was about to take an abrupt turn for the worse. Jamie and Kirk were squatting on the bank throwing pebbles into the river when Jamie pushed his brother in an effort to get back onto his feet. He didn't realise that his strength would push Kirk into the deep water. I don't think I've moved so fast in all my life. All I saw was Kirk's legs disappear into the river and then I screamed and jumped straight into the water after him. The river was choked with weeds and I was scared they'd pull him under. I managed to grab him and pass him to Kelly as I struggled to get out. But because I had heavy denim dungarees on, the water weighed me down and I found it almost impossible to get back onto the bank on my own. David arrived with his new girlfriend, Sarah, just as Mum helped me drag myself out of the water. Thankfully Kirk seemed OK, but we were worried in case he'd swallowed some of the stagnant water and I was convinced he'd get an infection. When Mum told David he wasn't at all bothered, and didn't seem concerned or offer to help. That was typical of the way he managed to remain completely removed from any normal situation. Later that afternoon the local A&E confirmed that Kirk was OK, but the day was ruined.

Life was just getting harder because every moment of every day was poisoned by David's presence. I couldn't sleep at night thinking he was under the same roof as Kirsty. But how could I get Kirsty out of there without telling her what David had done to me? Kelly didn't even know she was my daughter! I knew every nightmare scenario could be resolved if I only told everyone the truth, but I was caught in a tangle of my own secrets. The lies I'd been telling seemed so much more believable than the horrible truth. It really did seem impossible – I had no idea how to break my silence and I had no idea if I had the strength to confront the darkest scenes from my past again. Whenever David was around I didn't feel like an adult and mother

– I felt like that twelve-year-old again, vulnerable and petrified.

One night in autumn 2004, Mum told me that David had gone to a friend's house, so I allowed Alicia and Sam to stay over. I'd barely been letting them out of my sight, but for once it seemed safe to let them spend time at my mum's house. I was wrong. The next morning Kelly and I were walking up to my mum's to pick them up when the girls came running towards us. My heart almost fell to the floor.

'What's happened? What's wrong?' I shouted, mad with worry.

'Calm down, love,' Kelly said, but I shushed him and waited for my girls to speak.

'You were right, Mum,' Sam said. 'Uncle David is horrible.'

I thought I was going to be sick, but she carried straight on.

'We were just playing in the living room and he had a right go at us because we were distracting him from his computer.'

'Typical,' Kelly said, and turned round to go home, but I'd gone completely white.

'Hang on,' I said. 'Did David sleep at Gran's last night?'

'Yeah, he must have come back in the middle of the night,' Sam said casually.

My blood reached boiling point. I couldn't think, couldn't breathe.

'Oh my God!' I murmured.

'It's OK, Vicks,' Kelly said. 'Nothing happened – he only shouted at them.'

But I was seeing red. I'd had enough. I was shouting and swearing in the middle of the street.

'I can't take this anymore – I just can't do it. He can't rule my life like this, my girls' lives, and it has to end!'

I felt like I was going to self-combust. I was crying and screaming and pacing on the spot. Kelly was as confused as ever and didn't know what to do to help.

'Kelly, go and get Kirsty and bring her back to ours!' I screamed, and stormed back to the house with Alicia and Sam. Without a word of explanation I sent them to their rooms.

Kelly must've only been gone minutes but it felt like hours. I was pacing the living room waiting for them to come back with all kinds of thoughts going around in my head. The question that I couldn't get away from was: Will I have to tell Kelly the truth? This nightmare situation had finally gone too far. I'd spent months making sure that the girls only passed David on their way in or way out of the house, but knowing they had all slept under the same roof as him left me ice cold. What if he struck again? What if he was building up to something, waiting to pounce? Tears stung my eyes: it was all too dangerous. I began to resolve, deep down, that the time had come to finally reveal the terrible secret I'd kept to myself for almost twenty years. I knew life couldn't go on like this any longer. I felt like I was on the verge of a nervous breakdown. What if David stayed around for months, years even? How could I keep him away from my girls? The thought was torture. But I'd kept the secret to myself for so long that I genuinely didn't know how to tell it, how the words would come out of my mouth. I tried going over and over it in my head: 'Kelly, I have something to tell you'; 'Kelly, there's a reason why I hate David so much'; 'Kelly, I was raped' but none of it felt possible. It was like the words were attached to a cord that was being pulled back inside my throat. Or like David's hands were around my neck again.

What if he didn't believe me? Even if he did, I was also anxious about the outcome: what if Kelly was disgusted and ended up leaving me and the children alone and vulnerable? My head was full of paranoid thoughts, but deep down I was sure Kelly would stay around no matter what. We'd been through so much since we met that he had already proven himself a rock. He was the man I'd always dreamed about, who would take me in his arms and look after me. The more I thought about it, the more I became convinced that Kelly would react in the right way and really be there for me. Yet just thinking about telling someone was the furthest I'd come in years. There was no turning back now. I had to speak up for my girls' sake.

But what about Kirsty? And Mum? How were they going to take the news? I'd fobbed Kirsty off for years, saying her father just didn't want to know. Now I'd have to admit I'd lied to her. To everyone. How would she feel? Would she hate me? I was confident Kirsty and I had a close relationship – a lot closer than other mother–daughter relationships I knew – but would we survive such a shocking revelation? It would make her feel so tainted. Not only would Kirsty have to come to terms with the fact that she's the result of an incestuous rape, but also that her father is a killer. Was it worth it, destroying her world like that? I'd thought about it for so long, but I knew I had no choice. I'd been running away from David for too long. Now I had to face the truth front-on, and deal with the fall-out.

I worried that Mum would find it the hardest, though. She was one of the main reasons I'd never told anyone before. She adored David and since Dad's death she'd seemed much more fragile. Would she believe me, even now? But, after all these years, I had to take the risk. And I wasn't alone any more. I wasn't a little girl who was scared she'd be accused of lying. With Kelly by my side I'd stand my ground. Once the truth was out, things would never be the same again. But that would probably be a good thing. The strength in me began to build bit by bit the more I thought of the next step.

Then, I heard the door go.

'We're back, Vicks,' Kelly shouted.

Kirsty went straight upstairs to be with the girls and Kelly came into the lounge and gave me a big hug.

'Kelly, there's something I have to tell you,' I stammered.

15

Truth Must Out

That afternoon the sun blazed through the window, but inside the room I couldn't stop shivering.

I sat down on the sofa but I just couldn't seem to get started on what I wanted to say, so Kelly went to get me a drink while I composed myself. I could hear the girls upstairs, whispering and giggling – they knew something was going on, but obviously had no idea of the seriousness of it. I was terrified that telling Kelly was the wrong decision and of how this was all going to affect Kirsty. But it had to come out; life couldn't carry on as it was.

Kelly sat next to me and waited. He didn't say a word. I think he'd always been waiting for the moment I'd finally tell him why I was the way I was. Then, the words left my mouth so quickly that I don't even know what I said. I started crying and Kelly kept hugging me.

'Kirsty's David's,' I mumbled. I sobbed and sobbed, and random words like 'Rape', 'Kirsty' and 'David' left my mouth, but, thankfully, Kelly managed to piece the story together without me having to go into too much detail. I watched his face for a reaction and I didn't see any sign of disgust. In a moment like that, someone's facial expressions say a lot – Kelly's were full of hurt and pain for me, but there was no judgement, no disbelief. I'd suspected Kelly had battled with the reasons why I was the way I was for years, so I don't think it took him long to figure out what I was saying. It all made a horrible sort of sense for him.

'Oh, Vicks.' Tears filled his eyes as what I was saying sunk in. 'That bastard! That fucking bastard! My poor girl. How could he do that to his own sister? You were Alicia's age. A child! I'm so sorry, love. He'll never hurt you again.'

He wrapped his arms around me and held me close. I was hysterical, and I found it hard to breathe. I was just crying and crying as Kelly held me. I could feel the vibration of his sobs and for a few minutes we just held one another and didn't say a word. I knew he felt my pain; he was crushed by the weight of the secret I'd carried with me for so long.

What I most remember of that moment is the instant release I felt. My body unwound as the words left my mouth and I felt an incredible lightness. I could feel my body untighten; it was what I'd been praying for for years. I'll never forget the feeling of complete relief, like someone had taken a heavy load off my back. It was a physical release. At long last I felt I could finally relax, because I knew Kelly would now help me sort everything out. He was that type of man: very protective, and manly. Although it sounds selfish, it was a lovely feeling able to put my worries onto someone else's shoulders. Having carried my dark, poisonous secret around with me for so long, it was an amazing relief to be able to share it. I'd been waiting eighteen years for this moment.

Kelly and I were still holding one another tightly and crying when the boys barged into the room. We had to quickly pick ourselves up. That's what our home was like: never time to dwell on anything because the kids were there to distract us. Kelly just looked at me and whispered into my ear: 'I'll sort it.'

And I knew he would.

'Right, boys, off to your room,' he said, hiding his tears from them. After decades of bitter struggling on my own I finally had someone to help me untangle the mess David had made of all our lives.

Kelly knew that I'd never told anyone else. He didn't need me to confirm that this was the first time my secret had ever left my lips. For him, a massive jigsaw had just been pieced together, which explained where all my anger and self-doubt came from, plus my desperate need for love and my conviction that all I deserved was pain and betrayal.

But telling Kelly was easy compared with what had to come next. I couldn't even bear to think of telling Kirsty. My Mum's reaction worried me enough without even considering that.

'What will Mum say?' I asked Kelly. 'He's always been her blue-eyed boy. She won't believe me!'

'She'll have to. We'll make her,' Kelly said, stroking my hair.

I was getting myself worked up just thinking of what to say.

'I'll do whatever I have to,' Kelly vowed.

An hour had passed while we'd been talking, and Kirsty had slipped out.

'No!' I crumpled, when I realised she'd gone. 'How can I let her go back under David's roof?'

'I'll go to your Mum's,' Kelly said.

'Yes, we need to tell Kirsty now.' The tears were streaming down my face. 'What will she think of me?'

'Stay here and look after the children,' Kelly said. 'There's no way I can risk you bumping into David in this state.'

We had no idea where David was, but I was confident Kelly could look after himself. It was one of the reasons I finally told him. I'd been too scared of David to share my secret with anyone when I had to live alone with my children, but now I had Kelly I hoped he wouldn't be able to threaten or hurt me again. I knew Kelly would look after me.

I stayed at home, climbing the walls. Thank goodness I had the boys – they needed so much attention that there was no time to think of anything else. Yet I was so afraid of how Kirsty was going to react. Part of me felt I should've told her myself, but I hadn't even been able to tell Kelly properly – and he was the easiest one. This had to be handled so carefully. What Kirsty was going to hear would rock her to her very foundations and it couldn't be done by a blubbering wreck. She'd already lived through the death of her beloved grandfather, as well as my mum being hospitalised with depression. Kirsty was the one who mattered now and I needed to give her time to get over the shock before she had to face me.

Now I'd told Kelly, I felt that everyone should know. It was all or nothing. In my head I looked at it like a new scene, written into the script, which alters the direction of the entire film. Now the secret was out, it was going to change how all of us lived our lives.

I sat at home with a cigarette in my hand imagining how Kelly was going to tell Kirsty. He'd be telling her now, I thought. Right now the ground has collapsed beneath her feet. Will she be crying now? Will she hate me?

Over the next few days I pieced together the following events as painstakingly as a detective. I needed to know what they said, how they looked – how my family coped with this devastating bombshell.

Mum was in the living room and Kirsty was in her bedroom when Kelly arrived. He sat down next to Mum, made sure David was out, and said: 'I've got something to tell you and it's going to be hard, but it'll explain all the problems between Vicky and David.'

Mum looked confused but she listened as Kelly began. His voice faltered, but he made himself get the words out.

'Well, the most horrific thing happened . . . I don't really know how to say it . . . David raped Vicky.'

Mum didn't move for a while. She looked like she was in complete shock.

'What? I don't understand. My David? No . . . he wouldn't do that. It's not possible. Vicky? My daughter, Vicky? Who said it was true?'

'I'm so sorry. Your son, David. Your daughter, Vicky. He raped her when she was a little girl.' At that, Kelly said a look of sickened understanding spread across Mum's face.

'My God. Vicky. It's true, isn't it? David did that to her. It all makes sense,' she murmured. 'The last few decades all make sense.' Mum laughed a bitter, hollow laugh. 'How could I be so blind? She hated him so much. She couldn't bear to be in the same room. Couldn't bear him to touch her.' With that she broke down completely, sobs wracking her body.

'I should have known. I should have done something. But I never suspected anything so wrong, so evil,' she spat the words out.

After that, Kelly told me that Mum cried for ages. 'My poor little Vicky. She must have been so scared. Why couldn't she have come to me? All those times I made her go and visit him, she must have been sick inside . . . all the times I defended him . . .'

But the ordeal wasn't over for my poor mother. Kelly took a deep breath.

'There's one more thing. I'm sorry to have to tell you, but Kirsty is David's child. She doesn't know. She doesn't know anything.'

'No . . .' Mum cried even harder. 'Vicky was just a little girl. It's too much. How could he? I can't believe this is happening. And, my God, what about Kirsty? How is she going to cope? We've been lying to her all this time. Everything in her life is a lie . . . And Vicky's been struggling with this on her own?'

Mum later told me that all she could think about was how, while she was living her life, I must have been in constant turmoil. While she loved her son and tried to help him back on the straight and narrow, he had already committed unspeakable crimes against me. In that one afternoon she had to rethink everything she'd ever believed about her family.

'At least Len never knew,' Mum said, wiping her face with her hand. 'At least he was spared that. It would have broken his heart.'

Afterwards, Mum decided it was best if she told Kirsty herself. Kelly slipped outside to the garden to give them some privacy as Mum called her. Kirsty came bounding over, unaware of what lay ahead. But as soon as she saw Mum's face she knew something had happened. She sat down slowly.

'I have something shocking to tell you, sweetheart,' Mum said. 'It's going to be hard to accept. I've just found out too, and it was difficult to take in.'

Kirsty listened intently as Mum broke the news as gently as she could.

'I'm sorry, but when your mum was a little girl, something terrible happened. Something so terrible that she's been too scared to tell anyone the truth until now. Your father isn't who you thought it might be . . . Oh, Kirsty there is no easy way to tell you this, but your father is David. He . . .' She couldn't find the right words. 'He was very young, but he did something dreadful to your mum. It never changed how Vicks felt about you. She's always loved you. We all love you. So much. But you need to know what happened.'

Kirsty didn't move at first. She stared into thin air.

'Kirsty, are you OK?' Mum checked.

'Is it true?' she whispered.

'I'm so sorry.'

Mum wrapped her arms around Kirsty but she was rigid with shock.

'But it doesn't change anything. You're still my lovely girl. I promise you.'

Kirsty started crying.

'Poor Vicky,' she sobbed. 'I can't believe she's been carrying that secret around with her for so long.' She later told me that it took weeks for the revelation to sink in properly and, at first, she was just upset for what I'd been through. It breaks my heart to hear that – she is such a kind, giving girl and just didn't deserve any of this horrible mess.

Mum hugged her tightly and cried with her.

'I know it's hard to take in. I didn't know until just now. But we'll stick together. We'll all be OK,' she promised.

'And to think I was so desperate to know who my dad was!' Kirsty sobbed.

Kelly came back inside and, seeing them both sobbing, wrapped his arms around the two of them.

Eventually they looked up and came over to see me. It was the moment I'd been dreading since the day I discovered I was pregnant with my brother's baby.

I have no idea how long I waited but it was early evening by the time I heard the door open. At the sound of it I jumped up and began pacing round the room. I was so nervous of meeting their eyes, and admitting to them face to face what had happened. When they walked in the room I just stood there, and then I started crying again. Mum came straight to me and hugged me.

'I'm sorry you couldn't tell me,' she said.

Then my beautiful Kirsty came in and ran into my arms. We fell back onto the sofa and hugged and cried for ages. It felt like hours. No words left our mouths; we just held one another close.

That night, Mum went home, but Kirsty stayed and we all slept under the same roof. Well, we all went to bed, but I don't think any of us slept. I certainly didn't; I lay on the bed and cried. Kelly lay next to me and talked gently to me for hours. Usually I shrugged him off, but for once we lay in bed with our arms around one another, wondering what the morning would bring.

As soon as we were up the next morning Kelly texted an officer at Mosaic, which is a housing support network in London and Essex. Although they mainly deal with home-related issues we knew they offered support for any problems. We didn't know whom to call, but we desperately needed advice. Kelly suggested talking to them because they had been a fantastic support to us in the past with other general day-to-day problems, so we trusted them to give us good advice. It didn't seem right calling the police as it happened so long ago. Plus we didn't like the idea of officers in uniforms flooding into our home. The Mosaic officer called Kelly and he told her that a serious offence had happened in the family and we needed to see some senior officers. They said they'd send someone round as soon as possible. And then we waited.

Then, just as Kelly put the phone down, Mum called.

'David's gone missing,' she said.

16

Numb

It was like I'd been hit by lightning. I couldn't speak and I couldn't digest what Mum was saying so I handed the phone to Kelly. I watched as he spoke to her and I could tell from his body language that there was some more awful news to come. I held my breath and waited for him to put the phone down.

Kelly's face was exhausted when he finally turned to us.

'Something terrible has happened. It looks like David's kidnapped a girl.'

I felt my legs go from under me, and I collapsed onto the sofa.

A policeman had knocked on Mum's door that morning asking her if she'd seen David. The officer explained that he seemed to have abducted an ex-girlfriend, Sarah, and that no one knew where they were. Sarah had gone out with David for a few months. I don't know how they met but she was a pretty girl from a solid, middle-class background. Mum had told me that they'd split a while back, but I had just been relieved that she'd got away from him before he could hurt her. Turns out I was wrong. Turns out David had gone round to Sarah's house for a chat the previous evening, but when she got into his white van to talk to him he just drove off. Her parents reported her missing when she didn't come back that night.

I could feel hysteria mounting inside me as the story came out.

'So no one knows where they are?' I asked. It made everything so much worse. I felt terrible for Sarah, remembering what had happened to Helen all those years ago and the feel of his hand on my throat. What would stop him hurting her too? At the same time I was beside myself with worry about my children.

'What if he comes here?' I asked desperately. 'What if he does something?'

Kelly put his arms around me. 'I won't let him, don't worry. I'll do something,' he said.

I had to believe him. I'd finally told my secret. There was nothing else I could do.

Within just a couple of hours, two senior workers from Mosaic were at my front door and so we quickly sent the girls to their room. Kelly had already taken Jamie and Kirk to school, thinking it was for the best. He told the teachers what had happened and asked them to keep a close eye on the boys.

The Mosaic officers already knew David was on the run; they seemed very worried and put me in touch with Brentwood Child Protection Unit (CPU) to get the ball rolling, as the CPU was going to take a statement, so we could start the proceedings. In the end, it all happened so quickly that I can't remember who dealt with what. But it was still morning when an amazing woman called Susan Clarke from CPU arrived. She explained that they needed to take a statement and that I had to go with them to their interview rooms.

That afternoon I went to Stamford Police Station where they had a section built for more informal interviews, with sofas and coffee-making machines in each room. As we arrived I was very nervous. I couldn't stop picking at my clothes. Would they believe me? With Sarah still missing, would they blame me for what happened, for not speaking out earlier?

Kelly wasn't allowed inside the interview room with me; but he was allowed to sit inside a video room next door, so that he could make sure I was all right. I sat on a sofa with a drink in my hand, facing a couple of professional-looking women. I didn't know what to say. I was still scared but I also felt that somehow the tables were slowly starting to turn. David had had such a hold over me for years, but now he was the one who was panicked and on the run. I felt like he had nothing over me any more.

The women at the CPU were very sensitive and didn't rush me at all, but eventually they started gently asking questions. 'If you can start by telling us what happened yesterday,' they said. I took a deep breath and started to talk.

At first I couldn't get the right words out. I kept stumbling and saying the wrong thing, completely flustered. 'I'm sorry,' I said, again and again. I'd spent eighteen years locking the words away and even though I'd told Kelly, I'd never had to go into detail before. He'd worked most of it out for himself, so I'd only had to confirm the horrible truth. As Kelly told Mum, and she told Kirsty, I still hadn't had to speak about it. It felt like I had to physically allow the words out of my mouth. It actually felt like something was being unravelled inside of me. But, in time, I began to tell myself that it should be easier telling these women because they were strangers. I didn't have to worry about how my secrets might hurt them.

Eventually everything came spilling out – the horror of the rape, the disbelief and sheer terror of all the years that followed. The women only asked a few questions regarding the details that I found most difficult to talk about, like the rapes themselves. It was hard reliving it, and completely mortifying. I had to admit how he abused me, and even though it wasn't my fault, it was still humiliating.

I was in there for several hours as the women talked through everything with me. They were lovely. I didn't feel that the interview was too intensive: they asked me something once and that was it, nothing like the interrogation I thought it was going to be. It was like talking with trusted friends, and I only wished that my petrified twelve-year-old self could have found such sympathetic, non-judgemental listeners. I knew Kelly was watching next door too and, in a way, I was glad. At least I wouldn't have to go through it all again. Finally he would know everything.

After the interview was over it was explained to me that a DNA test would prove everything, so I didn't need to worry about telling them specific details about the rapes. We arranged for Kirsty and me to go along and get tested in a couple of days' time. A scientific test made it all seem so horribly real and official.

During the first two days I didn't see much of the kids because there were so many officials to see. Mum was very attentive to Kirsty, but she stayed in her room most of the time. I was desperate to be with her and make sure she was OK but Mosaic, NSPCC and CPU officers were coming round all the time and asking a lot of questions and explaining procedures. It was pretty intense and chaotic. David and Sarah still hadn't been found, so, after years of silence, it was suddenly an urgent matter to get everything into the open. It felt like everyone was trying to help and do the right thing, but all at the same time.

I was desperately worried about Kirsty; I wanted to know how she was coping. She had had to deal with a huge shock, news that would change her life and her view on everything. However, like I say, we'd never been a talking family. We've never openly discussed our feelings or emotions so sitting quietly in corners and dealing with our own confusion was normal. I wish it was different, but I couldn't imagine anything leaving my mouth that could possibly help ease the pain my beautiful daughter was feeling.

Thankfully, Kelly was flitting between Kirsty, Mum and me, checking we were all doing OK and trying to encourage us to talk. He'd spend time with Mum, then come to me and tell me what she was feeling, and then he'd go to Kirsty and tell her how I was feeling. It was our way of coping and it seemed to work. The main emotion we were all battling was guilt. Mum felt guilty for not protecting me, Kirsty felt guilty that I'd carried a horrendous secret for almost two decades, and I felt guilty for causing them all such anguish.

'I feel like I've failed because I couldn't protect her and because she couldn't come to me when she needed me the most,' Mum confided in Kelly.

'There was nothing you could have done to stop David hurting her. You could never have imagined how dangerous he was,' he tried to reassure her, but Mum was adamant.

'Maybe, maybe not. But she should have been able to come to me when it happened. She shouldn't have had to cope with all this alone.'

As everyone got more and more worried about Sarah's whereabouts, Mum broke down again. 'I should have seen what he was like. I was his mother. How could I not have known?'

For Kirsty, things were even harder. After a lot of reassurance my beautiful girl told Kelly what was tearing her up inside:

'David's my father. What will stop me growing up to be like him? What if I destroy people's lives like he does?'

But she was seventeen and she had already grown up to be a fabulous young woman. Kelly tried hard to make her remember that.

'You're nothing like him, Kirsty,' he said. 'You've already shown how different you are by coming this far in life.'

But she wouldn't listen.

'I hate myself for being his daughter. You don't understand. I don't like myself any more,' she whispered.

I thought David had done his worst to me, but nothing I've suffered was as bad as hearing my gorgeous girl thinking she was as bad as her evil father.

Sarah and David still hadn't been found. A lady called Clare from Mosaic came round to see us every day to check we were OK and to update us. She was lovely and we felt we could completely rely on her to explain and sort everything out. She even took me to the doctors so I could get some anti-depressants to help my anxiety. Other than going to the doctors or police station, though, I didn't leave the house. I was terrified of seeing David and facing other people who might bombard me with questions. Gossip spreads like wildfire on our estate and I knew my neighbours were already suspicious of all the comings and goings at the house. And I was dreading sympathy. I didn't want people to look at me and feel sorry for me – I hated that. It was easier to lock myself away until they found something else to talk about.

While David was on the run, Kelly ran the house like a military operation. No one was allowed out of our sights in case he showed up. We couldn't risk anything. While I hid away, Kelly took the kids to school, picked them up, walked the girls to the shops, and picked up food shopping – no one was allowed to do anything normal. Knowing what a sexual predator my brother was, I was even more on edge about the safety of my beautiful girls. He was capable of anything. I was convinced he'd come and find us. Why not, if he felt like he had nothing to lose? What if he suspected I was finally going to tell the truth? Had he heard me shouting outside Mum's house? My head kept going over possibilities. I also wondered what else he'd do – would he attack any other young girls? Would he do anything to Sarah? Would I have blood on my hands for ever because I hadn't reported him earlier? My heart was in my mouth.

'Vicky, it's not your responsibility,' Kelly kept saying. 'He does whatever he wants to do. You can't be responsible for his actions.' But it didn't help ease the guilt I still felt. Even though I had genuine reasons for keeping my terror to myself, I still couldn't live with the idea that I might have stopped him if I'd only spoken out earlier.

Kelly often sat outside the house and watched the streets in case David came anywhere near us. He'd even warned neighbours and friends to keep an eye out for a white van and gave them photos of David so they could recognise him. I must admit, it made me feel a lot safer and I was very grateful.

Then, after three days, Mum got a phone call from the police. They had found David and he was in custody. The relief was immense, knowing he was now locked up and couldn't hurt us. It felt like our hellish ordeal might finally be over. Just knowing my rapist was behind bars gave me the opportunity to slow down and take in everything that had just happened. Now I could help my family pick up the pieces of our shattered lives.

But there were more horrors to be revealed. We heard from Mum that David had dropped Sarah back home after three days of horrendous abuse and then went on the run. He was finally arrested when police caught up with him in his van six hours later. Apparently he held up a pretend gun and aimed it at the police. It was claimed he wanted them to think he had a real gun on him so that they'd shoot at him. Before he was caught, he told a friend: 'I have to kill myself because I'm evil.'

Looking back, Kelly thinks David knew the secret was coming out when he took Sarah, as it would explain why he wanted to end his life. I locked myself in the bathroom when I found out. My worst nightmare had come true: I'd finally spoken out about David and he'd lashed out at whoever was closest. I'd stood up to him, so he'd found another victim.

The whole thing seemed too horrible to be true. While we'd been tied up giving reports to the police and social services, the newspaper had run reports about the kidnap and Sarah's parents had pleaded with David to return their daughter. She went missing on the Monday and she turned up on their doorstep on Wednesday, a damaged, terrorised girl. My brother had held her prisoner, raped her and repeatedly threatened to kill her. He'd kept her for one night in the van in a lay-by and then hidden her in a cheap hotel in Ely. No one knows what made him decide to release her. Apparently he told police that he wanted them to kill him. After everything he'd done to Helen, Sarah and his own family, it was hard not to wish they had.

Even though I was going through hell myself, I ached for Sarah. I couldn't imagine what he'd put her through and how she was going to get over it. I kept thinking that at least she was close to her parents and hoped that somehow they would help her through it.

Once David was behind bars, Kirsty and I had to give samples of our DNA so that the CPU and the police had solid evidence that David was guilty of incest. We had to go to separate stations so that there were no chances the swabs would get mixed up. At Grays Police Station I had a cotton bud scraped along the inside of my mouth and then placed into a sealed tube. That was it – it only took a few minutes. Kirsty had been quite nervous beforehand because she thought it involved needles and blood tests, and neither of us had realised it was so straightforward. That evening, Kirsty and I gave each other a hug, hoping that the worst was now over. If there had been any hope lurking in anyone's mind that David was not Kirsty's father after all, it would soon be quashed.

The next few weeks just merged into complete numbness. Now that David was in custody and had been refused bail we were able to relax, knowing he wasn't on the streets. We'd been concentrating so much on the interviews and collecting evidence against him that the full emotional impact of my revelation and David's crime hadn't kicked in. Now that was all finished, we had nothing to distract us and it was then that all of our feelings really reached boiling point.

Mosaic wanted us to go and see a counsellor but I couldn't imagine discussing our family problems with another stranger, especially when I'd kept it to myself for so long. It felt too soon. Mum went though, and she found it helped her see things differently. She saw a counsellor once a week for about three months. Although I had spent a long time being bitter that I couldn't tell my mum what had happened to me, I knew how hard it must be for her, hearing that her son had raped her daughter. Her beloved son had proved to be an utterly depraved and dangerous man who had caused horrible suffering to those he was supposed to love and protect. As a mother myself, I could only begin to imagine how that would make her feel.

Looking back, I suppose I could've made it easier for Mum by telling her that I didn't blame her at all for not seeing through David. But it wasn't that easy. To be honest, a part of me still felt some resentment towards her for keeping David in our lives. It was such a difficult time for all of us. More than ever I wished that Dad were here to help us get through it. But then I was also so grateful that he didn't ever find out the truth too. I can't bear to imagine what it would have done to him.

It also tore me apart thinking that Mum might still try to keep in contact with David after she knew what he'd done. After all, she'd stood by him after he was found guilty of Helen's manslaughter. But before any of us could ask Mum, Kelly made the decision for her.

'Look, I'm sorry to be harsh,' he said, 'But if you see or speak to that man again, you'll never see the children. We just can't risk it.'

'No, I won't see him,' she said quietly. 'I had no intentions, not this time. He's gone too far. I don't even know who he is any more.' With that she left the room and we all sat in silence. It was no pleasure to see the golden boy falling off his pedestal in such terrible circumstances.

A few weeks later, Mum came in when I was getting the kid's sandwiches ready.

'I got a letter from him. From David,' she said carefully. I put down the knife and turned to face her.

'What does he want? What does he say?' I asked. Was this it? Was Mum going to take my brother's side after everything she knew about him?

'Not much.' She looked me straight in the eye. 'I'm not going to reply.'

My heart flipped over with relief, but I tried to keep my voice steady.

'Really, Mum?'

'Vicks, I never thought I'd say this about my own child, but what David did to you was unforgivable. I know you think I always take his side, but after this I just can't be his mum any more.'

I nodded, and wrapped my arms around her, as if she was the child and I was the mother. We stood like that, not saying anything, for a long time.

I'm sure Mum has spent days, weeks and months wondering, like me, how David turned out to be so callous and disturbed. He was just seventeen when he raped me, little more than a child himself. Why did he rape a girl five years younger than him – and not just any girl, but his own sister? What could make a smart boy do something so terrible? I often wondered if anything happened to him as a child; had he been abused and none of us had known? Or maybe it was because he was so clever, but totally lacking in empathy? He had always loved control and to be the leader, after all. I remember watching him with his mates when we were young and they were all nervous around him. He would also turn on his girlfriends if they ever failed to do exactly what he told them. Perhaps he just raped me because he could? It was a power thing. He thought I'd never tell, so he did whatever he wanted to. That would've been the best buzz of all for him, just knowing he'd got away with it. For years it tortured me that I was allowing him to get away with it, but now, finally, he was caught. No reason can truly explain what David did to me, Helen and Sarah. For the sake of all his victims, he deserved to rot in jail.

While Mum was battling her own feelings of regret and guilt, Kelly and I struggled too. Kelly started drinking more and more and I was finding it hard to accept that I'd finally let it all out after keeping him in the dark for so many years. We were both trying to deal with so many emotions that we were struggling to cope. Kelly even started to feel guilty because he hadn't spotted the signs. We had gone through almost three years of hell and now he was punishing himself for not realising there was something seriously wrong with me. But no one could've imagined my secret. I tried explaining that to him but he wouldn't listen and, instead, he found solace at the bottom of a vodka bottle. In the end he went into detox for a fortnight because he needed someone to help him see the light and he wanted to be strong for me and the family.

'I'm sorry I'm being so weak,' he said. 'I'll get better for you.'

I gave him a big hug. 'Just concentrate on getting well. We want you back home.'

It was hard while Kelly was away because it was a time I really needed him, but I had to remind myself that all of this was hard for him too. While Kelly was in detox, he wrote me another one of his lovely poems:

I've spent my life going from day to day
I've done what I've done and I've done it my way
I've spent money however I feel
I've begged, I've borrowed, I've stealed
Then I met you and you changed my life
So I made the decision to make you my wife
Of all the decisions to make in the past
That is one I'm going to make last
You were the one who gave me your heart
And it was you who made my life truly start
So thank you for standing right by my side
And showing your love while I tried to hide
Because of you I'm seeing the light
Our future together is looking so bright.

I knew Kelly wouldn't let me down. He had a couple of weeks of feeling a low and vulnerable, but that wasn't surprising after the bombshell I'd dropped on him. I was confident he'd be back on his feet and by my side as soon as he could. I needed him more than ever now, because the tough times weren't over yet.

17

Struggling to Cope

It took about four months before David's trial reached court, and it felt like a year. I didn't go out at all for the first few months. Instead I become a total recluse, relying on Kelly to do everything for me: taking the boys to school, going shopping and running errands. I was nervous about seeing anyone, even people I'd once called friends. Part of me was embarrassed, ashamed of what my brother did to me and painfully aware that everyone now knew. I didn't want people to point the finger, stare, jeer, or even ask sympathetic questions. I just wanted them to act like nothing had happened and to leave us to work through our own problems.

Kelly told me he had made his way round the majority of people we had some kind of friendship with and told them the bare outlines, so that they wouldn't feel the need to ask me anything. But in our area there were people who weren't necessarily friends but who were still nosey and wanted to know personal details – it was those people I was wary of. I have always hated people talking about me behind my back, and I wasn't strong enough to deal with their wagging tongues. All I wanted was Kelly, and thankfully he filled the role of my knight in shining armour perfectly. In the best possible way, I think he quite liked being needed.

Thankfully the children went about their daily lives like nothing had changed, especially little Jamie and Kirk. The girls were a lot older, so they picked up on what Kelly and I were feeling and the tense atmosphere in the house. I also made a conscious effort to see Kirsty as much as possible but at the time I genuinely thought she was doing OK. Kelly gave her lots of opportunities to talk it through, but she never wanted to speak about it with him; until Kelly would bring it up she never mentioned her father and seemed to act like normal. I couldn't believe she was taking the news so well. I realised much later that I was very wrong, of course, and that she was obviously pulling the wool over my eyes. In public she still had a smile and a joke for everyone, but unbeknown to me, in private, behind her closed bedroom door, she was desperately struggling.

We'd informed the schools of what was going on at home so that they could keep an eye on the kids and make sure there was no bullying or teasing in the playground. Thankfully the children weren't subjected to anything like that. Even though I had to put up with a lot when I went out on the streets I was glad my children weren't experiencing the same torment. They'd coped with enough over the last few months.

As the court case approached I became more and more worried about the outcome. Mosaic, the CPU and the police officers kept telling me how convinced they were that David would be locked up for life, but I was sure he'd find a way of getting out of it. David had always been so intelligent – he could wriggle his way out of anything, so I was frightened he'd do it this time too. The police were very sensitive about everything, though, and instead of sending uniformed officers to the house all the time with updates they normally called Mosaic to inform us. I have to say the entire ordeal was dealt with very respectfully by the officials.

Still, I didn't have much faith in the justice system. As I was brought up in rough estates, I saw a lot of crime on our streets. Some idiots were found guilty and punished, but many got away with it. Seeing that happen over and over again during your lifetime doesn't fill you with much confidence, and even considering the magnitude of what David had done and the solid evidence we had, I still wasn't one hundred per cent sure he'd be properly punished.

It soon became obvious it was a worry we all shared. One evening Kirsty rang my house and Kelly answered. His face looked grim as he listened to the message. Hanging up, he turned to us and said: 'Kirsty thinks Mum's taken an overdose. She can't wake her up.'

I was numb at first. How much more could happen in our lives?

'Quick, go up there,' I said, while I gathered the children together. 'Hurry!'

Turning to my younger kids, I tried to calm them down. 'Don't worry now. Gran's a bit poorly, but Kelly will make sure she's all right.'

I hoped to God I was right.

When Kelly arrived he found Mum lying on the sofa with her eyes shut. Next to her was a pile of loose pills in an empty ice-cream box.

'Mum, can you hear me?' he called.

She started mumbling weakly.

Kirsty was nearly hysterical, but Kelly took control.

'Looks like sleeping pills to me,' Kelly said, counting up the empty packets. 'Thankfully, she hasn't taken too many yet.'

'What'll we do?' Kirsty asked. 'Shouldn't we call an ambulance?'

'I think she'll be OK. Last thing we want is for her to be sectioned again.'

Kelly made her drink lots of water and after a while Mum began to stir. He later confessed to me that he thought it was a cry for help, rather than a serious suicide attempt. I felt sorry for her because I think, as the years went on, she felt less needed and she was scared of being unwanted. She'd already lost her husband, and now her whole world had been torn about by the revelations about her son. When Kelly told me his suspicions, I admitted he was probably right. Whatever the case, it was a sharp reminder of how much Mum was hurting and how much she needed our support.

As I'd had a very mixed relationship with Mum for years, it was sometimes hard for me to sympathise with her. But I was her daughter after all and I hated to see her in pain. I knew she felt like David had betrayed her too. And maybe she felt like all her time loving him and giving him everything he ever wanted had been a sad, sorry waste of time. She was constantly telling Kelly how guilty she felt about not being there for me. It was obvious that she was also fighting her feelings of being a failure as a mother. As a mum myself, I knew it must be hard to face the fact that your own child had grown up to be a violent monster. How can you hate your own son? But, then again, if Mum had seen David's true colours much earlier in life, none of this might have happened. I was ravaged by so many questions and feelings of love and hate, but Mum had finally chosen us over David, and now she needed us. Kelly was very good with Mum and talked to her a lot. He was there for Kirsty too. Kelly had always been a good talker, as he was from an educated family who discussed their problems. I was used to shutting up and just getting on with things.

But it seemed that Kirsty and Mum enjoyed the chance to talk too and took full advantage of Kelly being there. I was glad they had someone to turn to; in a selfish way, it meant that I was left alone a bit more. But it became frustrating for Kelly; I was his wife and it was me he wanted to help more than anyone, but because I'd been so emotionally independent for so long, I wasn't used to opening up. We'd sometimes talk at 1am while we lay in bed, but that was rare. I still found it hard to sleep, talk or cry in front of anyone. Sometimes it still felt like David had cut me adrift from everyone I loved.

The fear of the trial made me into a physical wreck. I lost a lot of weight. If it weren't for Kelly making me eat for the sake of the children, I wouldn't have bothered. What made matters worse was that Mosaic officers were having to prepare me, in case I had to give evidence. They explained I'd have to sit behind a screen in court and answer questions. Even though I wouldn't have to look at David, the thought of just being in the same room as him was terrifying so I was building it up to be an awful nightmare experience before I even got there.

With all the pressure on us all, the relationship between Kelly and me began to become strained. He was such a support for the family that sometimes I forgot that he was a husband as well as a stand-in father, son and social worker. Amongst everything else, Kelly and I were still struggling sexually. I was finding it hard to let Kelly touch me at night because the rapes had resurfaced and everything was so clear again. And because he'd been so understanding it was easier for me to keep saying no to sex, even though I knew it wasn't helping our relationship. I knew he felt like he was treading on eggshells, wondering if he touched me the way David had or if anything he did reminded me of him. And, to make matters worse, I suppose I never did much to help ease his suspicions. I had slept with my back to the wall for as long as I could remember and now Kelly knew the reason why; he wanted to change me and help me, but it was hard to accept help after so long. David was waiting to hear his sentence, but I'd already been living with mine for nearly two decades.

These days I was crying a lot more than I had ever done before, though. It was like someone had switched on the tap and I couldn't shut it off again. Any moment I had alone tears filled my eyes and they got so full they'd fall. The tears had been locked away for so long it was like they were making up for lost time.

Thankfully, a few months before the court case, I was told I wouldn't have to give evidence because the DNA test results had proved David was Kirsty's father and it was enough to find him guilty. A huge weight was lifted from my shoulders. For a while I wondered if I should still go to court to see for myself the outcome, but I wasn't sure I could face everyone's eyes. I was the girl who'd had her brother's baby, and now everyone knew about it.

As the court date got nearer, I became an emotional wreck. It was like a roller-coaster ride: one minute I was coping, the next I was flat on my face.

In April 2005, on the morning of the trial, the atmosphere in the house was thick with tension. I'd finally decided I wasn't going and, after much deliberation, Mum also decided she didn't want to go. She didn't want David to see her and think she was there to support him so she decided it was easier if she stayed away. In the end we agreed to let a police liaison officer represent us. But Kelly thought it was best that he went, so at least someone faced the brute in court.

'You don't have to, love,' I told him. 'We could all stay away.'

'I need to go for you, and your peace of mind,' he said. 'Don't worry, I'll come and report straight back.'

Kelly wore the only suit he had, his wedding suit, and late that morning he drove to Basildon Crown Court. He later told me he was crying the entire journey because he was consumed with so much hate, and he was dreading seeing David. He texted me when he arrived and said my elder brother, John Paul, and Helen's family were there.

Kelly walked into court, sat next to Clare from Mosaic, spotted David and, after five minutes, he had to walk out again. He said he just couldn't stay. Before coming home, he drove to a lay-by and sobbed his heart out. I couldn't blame him. For the rest of the week we stayed at home by the phone and waited for updates from Clare instead.

The trial lasted five days, and David pleaded guilty to three counts of incest as well as kidnapping, rape, false imprisonment, threat to kill, dangerous driving and using an imitation firearm at the time of arrest. It was a shocking list of crimes, but he showed no remorse.

I remember the day we got the news of the verdict very clearly. We were all sitting by the phone at home waiting impatiently. Kirsty and Mum had come over too and we were all pretty tense. It felt like my entire life was resting on this moment. For me especially, it meant so much. Had it been worth speaking out against David? Was I going to have to see him ever again? It was terrifying. It felt like the result would end the chapter for me; it would be a signal for me to move on.

'What's the time? Shouldn't they have called yet?' I asked, staring at the phone and willing it to ring.

'It'll be OK, Mum,' Kirsty said, 'Clare will let us know as soon as the verdict's in.'

'I know, love,' I said, giving her a weak smile. 'I just want it all to be over.'

Next minute the phone rang and I shot to my feet. We all looked at one another, hesitating, and then I picked up the phone.

'Hello?' I said.

'Hi, Vicky, it's Clare.'

I dropped the phone like it had burned me, but Kelly picked it up.

'Hi, Clare,' he said. 'So, what's the news?'

We all watched his facial expressions closely. We could hear Clare's voice, but we couldn't make out what she was saying. After a few minutes, Kelly hung up and just looked at us.

'It's all pretty confusing, but it looks like he's got life,' he said, smiling.

But there were no cheers or jumping in the air. Yes, it was good news, but it wasn't news we could celebrate either. It wasn't like passing exams or winning the lottery – it was still a miserable day. But, no matter what, I was hugely relieved. It was the right outcome, one that meant I would never have to see my rapist brother again. We all sat in silence for a while and then Jamie and Kirk came barging into the room and interrupted the moment. I glanced at Mum and Kirsty and they were looking as blank as I was.

'I can't believe it,' I managed.

'Neither can I, love,' Mum said in a tired voice. 'Neither can I.'

But the story of David's trial had a nasty twist. After dinner we had another phone call from Mosaic and it seemed everything wasn't as clear as we had initially thought. The legal jargon was complicated, so when Kelly heard life sentence he clung to it, hoping it meant David would be locked up for good. Unfortunately, it was later explained to us that 'life' didn't really mean life. He'd got a life sentence with a minimum of twelve years in jail, depending on whether he passed his parole, which meant he'd possibly be back on the streets within a decade, or less, with good behaviour. It was also explained that he had received just three years for raping me. I genuinely couldn't believe it. Three years? His sentence was because of all his crimes combined, but the judge seemed to think the horror and turmoil he had subjected me to was only worth a three-year punishment, even though I had already served a life sentence. I was devastated and felt so let down. I just couldn't understand the justice system. But, more than anything, I was terrified that one day he'd be out again. David had already killed Helen, and subjected Sarah to an inhumane attack. How much more proof did the judge need to see he was a menace to society?

For the next few days there were articles in the newspapers about David's sentence, but, thankfully, in order to protect Kirsty, they didn't mention anything about the incest. It was all about the kidnap and Sarah. I felt painfully sorry for her and her parents. They'd been through so much already, and now the journalists were picking over her ordeal too, finishing off the humiliation that David started.

I had imagined that, once the trial was over, I could slowly piece my life back together and get on with living again.

But the verdict left a very bitter taste in my mouth and I found it hard to move on. I even questioned whether telling the truth had been worth it. I'd wrecked everyone's lives, but still David could be out in a decade and then the hell would start all over again. Kelly tried to convince me that I'd done the right thing. 'It was the only way forward,' he tried to reassure me. 'You would've carried on living a lie for the rest of your life otherwise.' But his words didn't make what I was feeling any easier.

In the days after the trial there were times I wanted to kill myself. The confusion and hatred that I felt inside was so deep that I couldn't go on.

One night I was in the kitchen, pacing the floor. I felt like I was going to explode. The kids were in bed and Kelly was watching television, but I couldn't settle. So many thoughts were going around in my head that I felt like I was going to faint. I looked at the knives, all clean and shiny in the kitchen drawer. I had never wanted to hurt myself so much in all my life. I wanted to pick one up and slice it across my arm. I just wanted some kind of exit for my pain and frustration, something to take it out on. It felt like nothing else I could do would help. I needed some kind of physical pain to overpower the emotional pain I was battling.

I said nothing to Kelly about wanting to hurt myself. I knew he wouldn't understand and that he'd take it personally, like he'd failed me or something. But I couldn't stop thinking that the knife held a new world of peace for me, the chance to sleep comfortably. It would finally give me closure. I even wondered if it would be better for everyone else if I were dead. The kids would never have an emotionally unstable mum again and Kelly would be free to find someone less damaged.

But I just couldn't do it. I was too weak; I just couldn't do that to my family. My kids were my everything; I couldn't leave them to fend for themselves in this world. And Kirsty was at such a fragile stage in her life and had been through so much already that I couldn't desert her now. Afterwards, I hated myself for even letting myself contemplate suicide. How could I even consider that? I hated myself so much. I was all over the place. In the end, I felt so much frustration that one night I picked up a knife and cut into the flesh on my arm. It was enough to hurt myself and release all the built up pressure inside me. I actually felt like a kettle when it boiled and whistled, as my body was holding so much inside that it felt like it needed an escape route for all the frustration. Other times, I hit my head against a cupboard – anything to try and alleviate the pain and bitter knots inside of me. It was my only way of bursting the pressure inside, and it was so hard to live each day with these knots inside of me that just wouldn't unwind. I was sick of trying and sick of battling them. I just wanted it all to end. But I didn't tell anyone; I couldn't dare admit I was a mess, and I needed to keep a strong front up for the kids.

Not everyone was fooled, though. Even though Kelly only saw the scars he knew what I was doing and it got so bad he even packed his things a couple of times.

'Why are you doing this to yourself?' he'd cry. 'I'm here for you, but you don't seem to see it or want it.'

'I know you are, but I don't know how to accept help,' I admitted. 'I'm sorry. I don't know what else to say.'

'I can't take much more of this, Vicks,' he'd sigh. 'I don't know how to help you and it's tearing me apart.'

He'd just about step outside the house with his bags before I went running outside after him. The thought of living each day without him tore me apart.

'I'm sorry, please don't give up on me,' I'd beg. 'I can't do this on my own.'

And every time he'd give me another chance.

But while Kelly and I were struggling to deal with the raw, disturbed Vicky who had resurfaced after the trial, Kirsty was also finding it hard to move on with her life. Initially, I had thought she was strong and was coping well. She never wanted to talk about David, though, and, when Kelly tried to speak to her, it took him ages to get her to open up. I was so consumed with my own problems that I couldn't see that Kirsty was sinking deeper and deeper into herself. I now bitterly regret not reaching out to her more, dragging her back into the heart of the family.

As the days and weeks went on, Kirsty began to spend more and more time in her room. She had been doing this before the trial, but now some nights Mum would check on her and find she had slipped out. Mum would call us, half-frantic:'I don't know where Kirsty is.'

'Don't worry. She's a sensible girl. I'm sure she'll be OK.'

Even as I said the words, I got a sickening sense of déjà vu. Kirsty was behaving just like I had at her age, rebelling against any authority. It was obvious that she had only managed to cope for so long and now everything had come tumbling down on top of her. Even from jail, David had the power to destroy lives.

Kelly felt so torn, trying to help us all. In the end, he couldn't cope and, despite my protests, decided to get me some professional help. One night, when I was crying in the kitchen, he came in with a very stern look on his face.

'Vicky, I'm taking you to Grays Hospital to get checked out,' he said.

I was hysterical. 'Please no, don't do that to me Kelly, please no,' I begged. I was very confused. I knew I wasn't coping, but I didn't want to leave the house either. As I continued to cry and throw things across the room, Kelly somehow guided me into the car. He buckled my seatbelt and called Mum to look after the kids.

'I have to do this, Vicky,' he said.

I cried the whole journey. I was so hysterical that Kelly had to stop the car and get himself some fresh air. He pulled over and parked at a lay-by and, within seconds of him sitting on the bonnet, I jumped into the driving seat and tried to drive away. I had no idea what I was doing – I couldn't even drive – but I wanted to go home. Kelly quickly stood up and I remember him looking so worried. He placed himself in front of the car and stopped me from moving. But, as he stood there, I struggled to get the car into gear.

'What the hell are you doing?' he shouted.

'Move, Kelly, please move,' I begged tearfully, as I was pulling on the gear stick.

Thankfully, I had no idea how to put the car into gear to make it move. I hate to think what I would've done if I'd succeeded. Kelly walked back over slowly.

'Move over, Vicks,' he said, sounding exhausted. In the end, we got to the hospital and they just prescribed some more anti-depressants. As if some fancy pills could put the shattered pieces of my life back in place! But, with Kelly's help, I determined to pull myself together. I'd broken my silence, and now it was time to finally break the hold that David had over me. My kids deserved to have a mother they could count on, and ultimately it was only me who could get myself through this crisis.

*　　*　　*

So much had happened by that stage that Kelly and I decided to move back to Tilbury after the court case in 2005. It was a joint decision – we needed a fresh start. We moved back to a council maisonette with a garden and, thankfully, it was a chance for Kelly and me to concentrate on family life. I loved my children, and my focus was on giving them everything they needed, even though I had gone to hell and back.

Soon after moving back to Tilbury, I got a horrific reception from the locals. Some teenage boys who had heard the gossip shouted at me from across the street: 'You asked for it' or 'I bet you enjoyed it', as if I'd wanted to be raped. It made my skin crawl. I couldn't believe how cold and selfish some people were. One woman cornered me in the street one day and said: 'You watch your back, lady. You should've kept your mouth shut. David will find you one day.' I had to just walk away. But it was this kind of reaction that I'd been dreading. Was I going to be labelled the 'girl that got raped by her brother' for the rest of my life?

I felt ashamed on Kelly's behalf. Was this the kind of treatment we were going to face for ever? People would want to ask him questions and I wondered how he was going to cope with that. Having been so private about everything for so long, it was hard accepting my life was like a soap opera to many heartless people.

18

Kirsty and Danny

As soon as we moved to Tilbury, our lives slowly began to balance out. Kelly and I spent all our time with the children, and social services slowly began to be less and less involved with our lives. Everything seemed to be on the up. Then we heard news of Kirsty that made me worry that our family would never escape David's poisonous influence.

One day Mum came round to the house and told me that Kirsty had started to stay out all night until the early hours and was mixing with a bad crowd. I worried, because it was so out of character, but I had confidence in her and hoped it was a phase that she'd grow out of. I'd always believed Kirsty was the sensible one among us because, despite everything, she had grown into such a fabulous young lady.

But instead of getting better the situation got steadily worse. While Kelly and I had been trying to battle with our own demons, we hadn't been paying enough attention to Kirsty's feelings and how she was coping with the news that her father was a killer and a rapist. Sadly, it soon became evident that she was losing control of herself.

Kelly's phone began to ring in the early hours of the morning. Kirsty's close childhood friend, Stephanie, was worried. 'Kirsty's legless,' she'd say, or 'You need to come and get her', she'd mumble on another night.

'Not again . . . Well, thanks for telling me, pet. Stay there and I'll come get her.'

Sometimes it was 3am when the call came, but Kelly always got out of bed and went to pick her up. She was drinking alcopops and vodka twenty-four hours a day, seven days a week. When I saw her so drunk, it brought tears to my eyes, because it confirmed my worst fears. My main worry when I told my family the truth about her father had been Kirsty reacting like this. But, as the weeks turned into months and she seemed to be managing, I suppose I lost focus and turned my attentions on myself. I feel terrible about it now. I let my little girl down and I'll never forgive myself.

It became obvious that Kirsty was turning to her so-called friends to try and block everything out. For the first time in her life, she didn't care about anything. She wanted to forget her own existence and, because all everyone she was hanging around with wanted was to have a good time, they didn't ask her about the gossip they'd heard on the streets.

On Kirsty's eighteenth birthday, I arranged a party at my house. I made food and invited all her good friends and family round. But she was late. We all waited and waited and then when she finally turned up she was already drunk. As it was summertime, she sat in the garden all night half-asleep, falling onto a friend's lap, completely out of it. I know most kids drink too much on their eighteenth birthdays, but it was clear that this wasn't just teenage rebellion. Kirsty had had a year of hell, and maybe she felt like she didn't have anything to celebrate.

While most of her mates seemed more than happy to ply her with booze, Kirsty's friend Stephanie was worried sick about her and confessed to us that she didn't know what to do to help. Mum tried talking to Kirsty and showing her how much she was hurting us all: 'It's just not like you Kirsty. You're better than this.'

'Am I?' Kirsty couldn't even look her in the eye. 'How can you say that when you know what my father did? Maybe this is exactly what I'm like.'

Mum wouldn't let that go. 'You're nothing like David – you remember that. You are a good, decent person. He was always in trouble, but you're totally different.'

It amazed me that my Mum had so completely changed her tune about her son, but Kirsty was too lost in misery and self-hatred to listen.

Kirsty began to hang out in filthy flats with addicts and drug-dealers. I even found out she was dating a drug-dealer for a while, but there was nothing I could do. Kelly and I were completely at a loss. Mum had never had to be strict with her before, and none of us knew how to discipline Kirsty after she'd been through such devastating times. While my eldest daughter was terrified about being like David, all I could see was how much she reminded me of me in my saddest, wildest days. It broke my heart, remembering how utterly alone I had felt.

I decided to move Kirsty back to our house so we could keep a closer eye on her, but, before long, she went back to Mum's and then she'd go missing again.

My daughter was in trouble, both emotionally and physically. I could see she was drinking herself to death and her head was all over the place. She was also allergic to alcohol, so it affected her more than other people. When she was six, she had stolen some wine from my fridge and drank the entire bottle. I rushed her to hospital and they diagnosed alcohol poisoning – which was pretty scary. Ever since, Kirsty's body has been very sensitive to alcohol. She knew this, but she didn't seem to care. It was agonising to watch.

I begged my daughter to see someone, to talk to a counsellor, but she wasn't interested. Occasionally she went as far as making an appointment, but then she wouldn't turn up, preferring to drown her worries in alcohol instead. It was like Kirsty didn't want to get better and straighten out her life. All she kept saying was: 'I'm scum, I'm worthless, and I'm going to turn out like him anyway.'

No matter how many times I told her it wasn't true, I couldn't get through to her. But, still, there was no way I was leaving her to fight this thing alone.

Kelly and I started spending three or four evenings a week in his seatless £100 white van driving round the streets looking for parties that Kirsty might have been taken to. When we found one, I'd take a deep breath and go off in search of my little girl, deaf to Kelly's warnings. Sometimes I'd walk in just when someone was coming on to her or feeding her more drink and I'd find myself physically pushing them off her and dragging her out. I know it's not an ideal way to behave, but it's the only way I could keep her safe. I hated acting tough but when I saw my girl in such a vulnerable position, I went into autopilot and my first instincts were to protect her. I had to make sure they knew they couldn't mess with me or my family. Kirsty was so intent on self-destruction that her guard was down and she was vulnerable. The idiots she was hanging around with were taking full advantage of her and I couldn't stand back and do nothing. At the time she hated me for it, but I couldn't leave her there.

*　　*　　*

Kelly and I were united in the battle to save Kirsty. It became obvious that we had the type of relationship that got much stronger in times of need. When the going was tough, we faced it together, and, in my eyes, that was good. We could both be irresponsible at times, but I was confident that when the going was hard, we were a solid unit.

But during the troubles with Kirsty, my other children began to suffer too. They looked up to Kirsty because she was the eldest and calmest. They loved her for always being so strong, so seeing her so weak was hard for them to accept. Sam and Alicia were worried sick about Kirsty, but I tried to encourage them to carry on being normal teenagers, telling them to go to the cinema and see friends in the hope it would keep their minds off their troubled big sister.

Meanwhile, little Jamie began to lose his temper a lot. He picked up on the stress in the house and reacted badly to it. His teachers began telling us that he was aggressive with the other kids in school and had started getting into fights. Thankfully, Kirk seemed able to zone out of our family dramas. I wish I could have said the same for the rest of us. It seemed so unfair that, even from prison, David could still have such a negative impact on our lives.

The children leant on Kelly so much that they started calling him Dad. The first time Sam called him that, it stopped him in his tracks and he got tears in his eyes. I looked at him and he was smiling – he was so pleased that they finally saw him as their father. It was like recognition for all his support through these difficult times. He was so happy he fell into a daze, mouthing: 'I can't believe it.' I was overjoyed that my children finally had the sort of father figure that I'd had: strong, reliable and full of love.

I just wished Kirsty could see that Kelly was more of a father to her than David could ever be.

We were all desperate to help Kirsty, but it seemed like nothing could break through her cloud of disgust and misery. Then one night she got so drunk that she hurt her little sister, Sam. They were playfighting but because Kirsty had been drinking, she didn't know her own strength and took it too far.

'Ow!' Sam sobbed, doubled over in pain. 'You kicked me! What did you do that for?'

'Oh my God. What did I do?' Kirsty turned white too. 'I didn't mean to hurt you. Are you OK? I'm so sorry.'

Hearing the shouts, Kelly ran in. 'What's going on in here? Sam, are you bugging your sister?'

'No,' Kirsty's voice wavered. 'It was me. I'm sorry. I didn't know what I was doing.'

Even though Sam was OK, Kirsty was devastated, and I think it made her see she couldn't go on as she was any longer. She had always adored her sisters and brothers, and being the oldest in the family meant she was used to protecting them. But being so drunk all the time made it hard for Kirsty to be responsible, and finally she saw that.

'I can't go on like this, Mum,' she said, when Sam had gone up to bed. 'You're right. I'm messing everything up.'

I gave her a big hug and promised to be there for her.

With the help of Mosaic, she started seeing a counsellor at a drug and alcohol centre called Cedar Project. The woman she met helped her see why she was drinking and, each week, she drank less and less, until eventually, after three months, she drank no more.

After the counselling Kirsty came on amazingly; I was so proud of her. She began to help Kelly and me with the other children and she became part of the family again.

I've always had a lot of faith in Kirsty and believed she's a strong person, who deserved better than the life she's subjected to in the area we live in. When she was younger, she never got into trouble like the other kids, and it proved to me how sensible she was, and how she managed to have the strength to turn away. But I could completely understand her setback. She had gone to hell and back with no idea of how to cope, and with me not giving her enough support because I was suffering myself into the bargain. It showed amazing courage and resilience that she managed to pull herself back. I want to be able to say I had some part in making her the wonderful young girl that she is, but I'm afraid I can't really take the credit. All I know for sure is that I am extremely proud of her and I know my dad would be too.

Kirsty began to think about going to college to train as a car mechanic. She loved motors, just like her Granddad, and was determined to make the most out of her life.

But fate had a different adventure in store for Kirsty. In early 2008 she met Joe and fell in love. They were smitten and Joe was a really good guy, with an apprenticeship as a labourer. I was pleased she'd found someone to make her happy, who could look after her. Then, just weeks later, she found out she was pregnant. It was a big shock because it was so sudden and unexpected, but Kirsty was over the moon. She had always wanted children – ever since I'd given birth to Kirk, she'd looked after him like he was her own. And she was very naturally confident around babies so I always knew she was going to be a brilliant mum sooner or later. She was twenty years old and having her first baby, and in our area that was pretty good! When I found out, I flung my arms around her. It was such exciting news after a very miserable few years. It felt like a fresh start.

Kirsty has always been so slim and petite so she barely had a bump throughout her pregnancy. It wasn't until she was six months' pregnant that she began to show properly, but her doctor assured us everything was fine. Slowly we began to prepare for the birth, preparing a nursery in Mum's house for her great-grandson.

But on 1 August, Kirsty suddenly started having problems. She was lying on the sofa at Mum's, nodding off in front of the television, when suddenly she felt a sharp cramp. Kirsty remembers moving about a lot in her seat, thinking it was indigestion, but when she mentioned it to Mum, Mum knew it was labour pains. An ambulance was called and Joe called Kelly.

'Vicky, we need to get to the hospital. Kirsty's gone into labour,' I heard Kelly shout.

'What?' I screamed.

Piling into Kelly's van, we raced over to Grays Hospital. When we arrived, Kirsty was in a labour room on a drip as nurses tried to keep her little baby inside of her. He was quiet for about twenty-four hours, but then he was ready to come out, three-months premature, and there was nothing the doctor could do to stop him.

I waited in the family room anxiously while Mum was holding Kirsty's hand. I didn't know where to put myself; my first child was in labour, and it was so overwhelming. Next minute, Joe came running out of the room.

'Vicky, she wants you now,' he said. I hesitated for a moment.

'Quick,' Kelly said, pushing me in the right direction. And we ran over as Mum came out. I grabbed my little girl's hand and stood behind her head at the end of the bed. I kept dabbing a cold flannel on her head and letting her squeeze my hand when she needed to.

Eventually little Danny Lee was born on 2 August, weighing 2lb 6oz. But poor Kirsty couldn't hold her precious baby, as he was whisked off as soon as he was born and placed in an incubator.

'He looked gorgeous,' I told her, stroking her hair. 'He'll be OK.'

I tried to sound as reassuring as I could, but inside I was panicking. Please God, don't take this one good thing from us.

It was so overwhelming seeing my daughter give birth herself. It was a beautiful moment and I was so glad to witness it. Here I was, a grandmother at thirty-three. It seemed strange that something so wonderful could come out of our terrible ordeal.

Over the next three months baby Danny slowly gained weight. Kirsty travelled about half an hour every day to see him and leave her milk. She had to use a breast-feeding pump to extract milk at first, but after a while her milk started to dry up so she reverted to powdered milk. But the hospital doctors and nurses were amazed with Danny's recovery and a month later he was 4lb 3oz and finally filling out his saggy skin.

As soon as Kirsty became a mother, I naturally saw her in a very different light. She was still my first born but she was now an adult. She just began to glow overnight, and became so confident and happy. I was just glad that my daughter could enjoy motherhood as a mature, confident woman, not a traumatised little girl like I'd been. If only I could have had Kirsty without the trauma beforehand. My love has never wavered, but I know that there were times when I've neglected her. I have a lot of regrets about that part of my life, but I just hope Joe will stand by Kirsty and Danny and treat them to the life they deserve.

Mum, Kirsty and I still haven't sat down and talked about what happened; I don't know if we ever will. I'm afraid of upsetting them, and I'm sure they're afraid of hurting me. We mention David's name and talk about his possible release dates, but we haven't mentioned what happened in the past. Kelly has spoken to them and told them what they need to know. There's still a strange silence at the heart of our family which may never be broken, but I'm glad Kirsty can talk to someone.

Kelly told me that, for a while, Kirsty was thinking of going to see David in prison because she had a long list of questions. But, in the end, she couldn't go through with it. She couldn't ever face him again.

Kirsty is testament to the fact that, whatever or whoever your parents are, you don't have to go down the same route. It took her a while to see that but eventually she got there, and now she's carving out a happy future for herself, and her little boy. When I see her holding Danny, it takes my breath away. I'm so proud.

19

Speaking Out

It has been a long journey since the days when I played with my beloved dog, Ben, as an innocent twelve-year-old in the pub garden, and it's hard not to get angry that I was silenced for eighteen years of my life. Fear, intimidation and uncertainty locked my secret within me, and me inside my secret. Watching David go on to hurt so many people only exaggerated my fear. He was showing me how much damage he could do, and, sadly, it worked. Every time he did something else bad, I buried the rapes deeper. Now my silence is finally broken and he's in jail where he belongs. For now.

But the hardest thing is that my journey isn't completely over yet. David has been in prison for three years now and the police liaison officers have told me that he's due to be considered for an open prison – for the last few years he's been held in a closed prison where there are security measures that stop the inmates escaping. Prisoners held in open prisons are called category D prisoners and can wander around the grounds and local town freely, but must show up for daily roll calls. There's an open prison near me in Tilbury What if he ends up there? I'll be devastated, as will the rest of my family, and my problems will start all over again.

I've started to dream at night about what David might do if he gets released. I have nightmares that he finds us and punishes us all individually. I don't believe he's learnt his lesson, and I don't think the last three years will have taught him anything. In my darkest moments I fear that he'll come out of prison wanting revenge and will not stop until he gets it. I may be a mother and grandmother now, but I'm still terrified of him.

It makes me sad that the judge thought that sending David to jail for three years was enough after taking away almost twenty years of my life. It seemed like such a terrible miscarriage of justice.

But I don't want the sentencing system to deter any victim of rape or abuse from coming forward and prosecuting their attackers. I wrote this book so that people can see the pain and misery I went through by keeping my secret to myself. At the time I was so scared of hurting my family, and of David hurting me, that it seemed like the only option. But, if anything, my silence let David offend over and over again, and let him destroy other families: Helen's and Sarah's. I have to live with that now; I have to live with the guilt that I could have stopped him years earlier before he hurt anyone else. I can't forgive him and some days it's hard to forgive myself too. I was a frightened little girl who cocooned herself away from reality. And I have no choice but to accept that now.

I'm not embarrassed about what David did to me any more. I'm not ashamed that, as a twelve-year-old girl, I was too scared to fight him off. I don't care who knows I was raped – if anything, the more people that read this book, the more it might help. There is no shame in being raped; it's not our fault. Whatever else you take away from this book, please believe that.

When I think about the times I almost told, I want to cry because I wish so much that I had found the words. The only comfort I get about not coming forward earlier is that my dad never had to know the truth. It's scant consolation, but at least he died without ever having to hear what David did to me.

If I've learnt anything, it's that victims of rape and sexual abuse need to find the strength to come forward and fight for justice. We can't let our attackers win. So please use my story as a lesson: that keeping a secret is not helping anyone, especially yourself. Please turn to someone you can trust and be strong. When you find that one person you can trust, don't miss the chance to speak. Otherwise the silence will poison your life and put other women and children at risk.

You start by locking up a secret inside of yourself, but you end up being a prisoner to it. One day I know that my children will read this book and understand the pain I went through, and hopefully it'll explain the times when I haven't been there for them. I hate myself every day for those times that I was too deep in my own pain to put them first. Now, I hope I'm a good mother to my children and that I can use my terrible experiences to help others.

My dream is to set up a helpline for all the children who have felt like me. I want to be able to reach out to everyone who has felt cast aside and intimidated. If this book helps even one person to feel stronger, to feel less alone, to finally speak out, then I'll have done what I set out to do.

After my brother put a brutal end to my childhood when I was twelve years old, I had no ambition or enthusiasm for life. All I wanted to do was to stay at home, to hide away somewhere safe. But now I see hope, and I can believe that life can get better. I've seen for myself that even though I went to hell and back I've come out the other end, survived it, and now I can plan for a very different future. I want to do something constructive with my life. I suppose writing this book has been one long counselling session and it's been a chance to re-evaluate things. I'm keen to get out into the big wide world now and see what I've been missing for so long, to mix with people, and to have fun. I'd really like to go to college and train as a complementary therapist and visit retirement villages. For the first time in my life, I have dreams for myself and not just my family.

I know I wouldn't have come this far, though, if it hadn't been for Kelly. He's become more than my knight in shining armour – he saved me and gave me a life again. And I've seen the hurt I've put him through; he's suffered too. He talks about it like it was his duty to help us, but I know for certain that many men would've walked away. He didn't. He stuck around and was there when the going was really tough.

This is what he thinks:

After Vicky broke her silence my entire life changed. I became so much more of a man. I grew up and I finally got to know the true meaning of responsibility. My life was nothing before I met Vicky, but she has made me see that no matter what you go through you can come out the other end a better person.

My main focus in life is my family now. If I'm not near them, I feel they might get hurt. I'm very protective.

There were so many times I thought I was going to lose Vicky. She was so low and depressed that I didn't know how to reach her and save her. But together we managed. It's made me see what real love can do. I was so scared at times – scared for Vicky, scared for myself and our family – but we managed to get through it.

I never once questioned my love for Vicky. There were times when I wondered if she loved me, but I was constantly trying to convince her that my love was genuine and that I wasn't going anywhere. Finding out what David did to her didn't change a thing. If anything, it made me love her even more, because I wanted so much to look after her and I wish I could've protected her back then. Even now, I get goose bumps on my body when I think of what she endured. At the beginning, I had to tell people what had happened, and every time it hurt, because I wasn't talking about a stranger, but my wife.

I have nothing but pity for David. He's a pathetic version of a man. Even though he tried to ruin his family's life, they managed to pull through. Instead, he's just ruined his own life. If he ever gets out, I will never let him touch Vicky or the girls. I will do everything in my power to make sure they never have to see him again.

It makes me feel proud that after eighteen years Vicky chose me to help her. She trusted me enough to tell me her deepest, darkest secrets and I'll never forget that. I just hope I dealt with it the best I could and that she was glad she chose me to help her.

Kelly and I are so much happier now. We talk and have fun. I can't remember the last time we had an argument. But we still take each day as it comes because every single cut isn't healed just yet.

The birth of baby Danny has helped us all to get excited about the future and move on, Mum included. As I'm still very busy with Jamie and Kirk, Mum goes with Kirsty to see Danny in hospital every day. She's very supportive, and loves being a great-grandmother. I should be thankful, but, after everything, Mum and I still have an occasionally strained relationship. I suppose that's understandable after everything we've been through, but it's proving harder for us to move on than I would like. I will forever be in Mum's debt for taking in Kirsty and helping when I couldn't be a proper mother, but over the years my secret has built a wall between us that is difficult to knock down, even now.

Mum understands why I don't want to talk about David, and has never asked any questions. Maybe there's also a part of her that doesn't want to hear what I have to say? I know I don't want to pry too deeply into Mum's feelings for my brother. Knowing how hard and how blindly she's always loved him, I find it hard to believe that she doesn't harbour secret hopes that he'll reform. I'm afraid that, after all he's done to me, to Sarah and to Helen, I could never think of my brother as anything but a monster.

My life was stolen from me when I was just a little girl, by one of the people I should have been able to trust most, and I had to battle with a dark, poisonous secret for the next eighteen years. I stopped playing with my dolls and had to prepare to be a mother. I couldn't do anything innocently, like normal girls my age; everything was tainted with horror and disgust. I learnt such bitter thoughts and feelings, a lot earlier than most girls ever have to, and I still feel angry about that. I used to watch other girls my age play and be happy and feel physical pangs of jealousy. I used to wish I could be transported back to the time before my brother raped me. But it never happened, and my desperate partying later in life was just a way of trying to get that carefree girl back again. So, when I see my girls being normal teenagers and doing all the things I never did, it's mesmerising. I love to chat to them about boys, fashion and school. In a way, seeing them so happy makes up for the youth David stole from me.

When I look at Sam, my youngest daughter, and I think how depressed and mixed up I was when I was her age, it still brings tears to my eyes. I can't imagine how any adult man would want to take advantage of such a vulnerable child. I imagine what I would do if anyone hurt Sam, or any of my children, for that matter, and I fear I couldn't be held responsible for my actions.

I suppose my ordeal has made me overly cautious of men and I worry about when my girls fall in love, as I can see how it makes them vulnerable. I want to wrap them up in cotton wool and protect them from everyone, but I know I can't. I've tried hard not to let my attitude to men rub off on my daughters, though, as they deserve happier lives, lives not ruled by fear.

If I could wish anything for my children it would be for them always to have someone to confide in, and to be surrounded by love. In some ways, my terrible ordeal has made me a better parent. My kids always get lots of hugs and kisses, and they know they can come to me with their problems, no matter what. No child of mine will ever suffer the way I did, crushed by a secret that they were too terrified to share.

For me, too, the story has a happy ending. I finally found my strength when I had Kelly by my side and I built up the courage to stand up to my rapist. I have no regrets about telling the truth. It was a long and hard emotional journey, but it was worth it. My life was born all over again the day I finally refused to be silenced.

Epilogue

The final words belong to my brave and beautiful Kirsty, who, in spite of everything, has turned into a strong woman and a fabulous mother, and the very best daughter a mother could ask for:

David always treated me very differently to my sisters when I was younger. When Sam and Alicia came round to see me at Gran's we used to always bump into him and so I noticed things.

If Sam or Alicia ever disturbed David, or woke him mid-sleep, he'd shout and get mad at them, but I knew from a young age he would never shout at me.

Sometimes I'd try and wake him, to test my theory, and he never said a word. As a child I thought it was funny, and felt privileged that I could do no wrong. I obviously didn't realise why he was behaving that way. To anyone else he was a very nasty and impatient man, but with me he was always chatty and quite kind-mannered. I thought it was just because I was the eldest and more mature than my siblings, and also because I lived with him and his mum. But when I found out the horrific truth everything made sense.

I remember, just before Mum's secret came out, I had interviews with the Prince's Trust to try and find a career path. I've never been a really confident person and so I was very nervous about the interview. In the end I worried myself sick and, when the ladies arrived at Gran's flat to meet me, I ran out of the house. I didn't know where I was going but ended up on a riverbank. Amazingly, David came after me and found me. He was so calm it was untrue.

'Are you OK,' he asked. 'What scared you in there?' He then helped me calm down, tried to teach me how to control my nerves and showed me some breathing techniques to help face the interviewers. By the time I got home the women were gone, but, with David's help, I arranged another appointment and met them.

Although it was obvious David favoured me, he also always made me feel very uncomfortable. It felt weird that he could be so nice to me, yet aggressive with everyone else. He was so unpredictable that his fits of kindness freaked me out. There was something creepy about him, and, as a child, I couldn't figure it out. He wasn't normal enough to be a typical uncle, but he was too distant to be a brotherly figure. He just didn't fit any particular role model; he was just David, the man who tried to be nice but whom my mother hated and who was always in trouble. He had this strangeness about him that no one could put their finger on.

I had spent my life wondering who my dad was. Mum had told me once that my dad was a boy the same age as her that she met on a caravan park. It was the tale she told everyone. But she went on to tell me that, because they were so young, he hadn't been ready to take responsibility for me. She obviously hated lying to me, but, by this time, she had told this lie to so many people, I think she had started to believe it herself.

I used to wonder if I looked like my dad. Did he have

dark hair? Did he ever think about me? But, as I hit my teens, I couldn't bring myself to ask Mum more questions. I knew she didn't want to talk about him and I didn't have the heart to ask. I never brought the issue up. I had a good family and a mother and grandmother who loved me, so I taught myself to forget about my father.

Then, when I was seventeen, my world fell apart. Finding out David was my father was the most complicated thing I'd ever felt: a mixture of shock, revulsion and a sense of things fitting into place. I'd always wanted to find out more about who my father was, but when I did it was the biggest disappointment possible. I couldn't get my head around what I was being told. I hadn't just found out who my father was, but also that he was my uncle and that he had raped my mother. I begged there to be some mistake, but Mum obviously knew the truth.

At first I cried tears of shock that I finally knew the real story. But then they turned to tears of pain for my mother. I loved my mum so much that the thought of her being raped made my skin crawl. I couldn't accept that she had suffered so badly, so I suppose I dealt with the information in different stages. At first all I could digest was that Mum had been raped; I pushed my own feelings aside, and instantly thought of Mum and what she must've gone through. It must've been horrific for her. It felt simpler to deal with it from her perspective, feeling more sorrow for her pain than mine. I completely understood why she had kept the awful news to herself for so long. How do you find the words to tell that sort of secret?

I sometimes wonder whether I would've preferred

never to have known who my father was, but I still can't truly answer that. I know Mum was struggling to cope and live her life as it was, so it was her only option in the end and, thankfully, it has brought her some sense of peace. I can accept that Mum's lies were there to protect me and I have no bitterness towards her for that. Now I have my own baby, I understand that need to keep them safe from harm at whatever cost. She did what she thought was best and I could never hold that against her. She was just a child when it happened, after all.

To start with, so much was going on with the court case that it was easier to continue pushing my pain aside. Whenever I was alone in my room, though, I'd begin to think about David and I'd feel bitter hatred and confusion. It was impossible to think of him as my father, so I'd cast aside my own feelings and think about Mum again – it was easier. But, as time passed, I couldn't contain my personal heartache any longer.

Every time I thought about David, I'd think back to my childhood. It all made sense now, why he had been so nice to me, why he had treated me so differently, but also why I was never able to work him out. The last thing I had ever suspected was that he was my father. He was an evil rapist and killer and I was his daughter.

As everything sunk in, I was left feeling cold and disgusted. What would people think of me? Would they hate me too? I started to wonder if I'd turn out like David and if I was destined to a life of crime and violence. His blood was running through my veins. Was I a ruthless, heartless person like him? While I'd been worrying about Mum, I'd purposely forgotten about me and my feelings, but slowly I began to feel consumed by anger and self-hatred just for being David's daughter. I started to really despise myself.

But Mum and Gran helped me feel strong and eventually I began to see the truth: I was nothing like David.

'You are your own person, Kirsty,' Gran said. 'You are in charge of your life.'

I began to believe it was up to me to decide how my life turned out. I made a promise that, whatever David was, I would never be the same.

I'm more scared of David now than I was when I was a child. At least when I was a little girl I didn't really understand what he'd done to people. Now I know the true extent of what he's capable of and it terrifies me. Part of me wants to talk to him, to get some answers out of him, but I've coped without a dad for this long, and I know I'm better off without him. Like Mum, I never want him back in our lives.

I still spend the odd moment thinking about everything that has happened to us as a family, but it's getting less and less as the years go on. I just want to get on with my life. I'm a mother myself now and I see life very differently. My son means the world to me; he's my main priority in life. Becoming a mother has helped me see why Mum loved me from the moment I was born, even though I was the product of her rape. Giving birth is a loving act and the love that is born is more important than anything else. I understand more now why Mum kept her secret for so long. She tried to protect me and I would do the same for Danny.

Once, I wanted to end my life and escape all the pain and confusion, but I've grown up so much. Danny is my life now and all I want is to enjoy my days with him.

David is a distant memory and has nothing to do with our family now. I hope he rots in prison.

Love of a family is priceless and my mum loves me dearly. I only hope Danny will grow up feeling as loved by me as I have felt loved by my Mum.